D0793897

DATE DUE

JUL

7 9

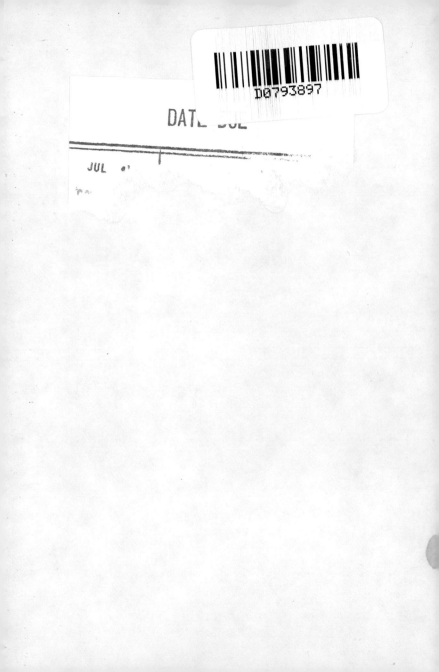

AFRICAN WRITERS SERIES
Editorial Adviser · Chinua Achebe
78 Short African Plays : Cosmo Pieterse

Short African Plays

Edited by COSMO PIETERSE

HEINEMANN
London · Ibadan · Nairobi

822

Heinemann Educational Books Ltd

48 Charles Street, London W1X 8AH

P.M.B 5205, Ibadan, P.O. BOX 25080, Nairobi

EDINBURGH MELBOURNE TORONTO AUCKLAND
HONG KONG SINGAPORE KUALA LUMPUR NEW DELHI

ISBN 0 435 90078 1

© Heinemann Educational Books Ltd 1972
© Preface and Notes Cosmo Pieterse 1972
First published 1972

All rights whatsoever in these plays are strictly reserved and on
no account may performances be given unless permission has
first been obtained from one of the offices of Heinemann Educational Books Ltd listed at the top of this page

Printed by Cox and Wyman Ltd,
London, Fakenham and Reading

Contents

c. 1

Acknowledgements

Acknowledgement is made to the following magazines and broadcasting services where plays were first broadcast or published:

Kofi Awoonor's *Ancestral Power* and *Lament* were first broadcast on *Deutsche Welle* on a Transcription Features Services production.
Cosmo Pieterse's *Ballad of the Cells* appeared in *Journal of New African Literature and Arts*.
Mbella Sonne Dipoko's *Overseas* was first broadcast in the BBC African Theatre.
Ngugi Wa Thiong'o's (James Ngugi's) *This Time Tomorrow*, first broadcast in the BBC African Theatre, was also published by East African Literature Bureau in *Three Plays* by Ngugi Wa Thiong'o. David Lytton's *Episodes of an Easter Rising*, was first broadcast on the BBC Third Programme.

I should like to thank, again, all the authors for their co-operation and patience, and the publishers, especially James Currey, for outstanding, much-enduring forbearance and assistance, and to express my indebtedness to Dennis Duerden of the Transcription Centre, London and *Deutsche Welle* as well as to John Gordon of the BBC African Theatre for invaluable advice, opportunities and material.

Preface

Of the ten plays collected here, all but three have
been performed – as readings; on radio; or on the stage.
Of the three hitherto unperformed ones, one has notes by
the author himself. In the case of my own play, the rather
copious notes I had intended to add, not only as an editorial indulgence, but also because of the prompting of
three British readers and one fellow-South African who all
felt that these were necessary for readers not versed in
material brought into play, have been dropped in favour
of the more generally useful material. Short biographies
and character lists head the plays.

For this volume I have dispensed with any form of
critical annotation; instead, to assist the director browsing
for a suitable play, there is a brief summary of scenes
and a synopsis of themes and/or events to cover each play
at the end of this volume.

Each of these plays was chosen for itself: hence there is
an interesting (one hopes) variety of spirit, setting, style
and story. Quite coincidentally, the book itself seems to
have become a unified and integrated volume. This is the
more striking – though not strange – when one considers
the two spans of time covered by our plays. With regard
to composition, the time-span ranges from July, 1962 to
a revision date in February, 1970; and as regards period
covered by the events of the plays, time ranges from the late
nineteenth century to the late 1960's. The geographical
range that is covered is an equally wide one: five West
African plays and two from East Africa and three from

South Africa, with authors on the whole exploring those areas of country they themselves come from. We regret not having been able to include translation from Arabic plays; a further volume will hopefully contain work from the U.A.R., the Sudan and the Meghrib. Fortunately it could again contain stage, radio and film (T.V.) plays, as well as an author's dramatization of his own short story.

It is remarkable that despite 'randomness' of selection and a fair variety of style, etc., quite a definite poetic mode and a strong tragic mood should have established themselves quite firmly in this volume. There is no space to expand on this phenomenon here, except to remark on the ritualistic spirituality of this mode-mood that cleanses as it activates and recreates, that purifies as it pains and persuades, so that the final effect is the achievement of resolution and the shaping of resolve.

Finally, then, one can only express the hope for this volume that (amongst a multitude of other wishes for it) in essence it may be found useful, stimulating, interesting, and provocative!

Cosmo Pieterse

Ancestral Power

KOFI AWOONOR

Kofi Awoonor *was born in Wheta in the Keta district of Ghana. He published in 1964* Rediscovery, *a book of poetry, and another collection* Night of my Blood *was published recently in the U.S.A. He has taught in colleges, researched in African Literature, acted on the stage, been Director of a film company and written for radio. He is now Professor in African Literature at the State University of New York, Stony Brook. He has co-edited* Messages, *an anthology of Ghanaian poetry in English, and has published a novel,* This Earth, My Brother.

CHARACTERS

Akoto ⎫
Goku ⎬ *two men of about middle age*
Police constable

Set near a Ghanaian village
in modern times

2

AKOTO : Hey, you canoe which the hippo cannot upturn,
where are you going, your heels not touching the
earth?

GOKU : That is my name. The name which says it was
within its shell and yet became a source of trouble
to the elders. (*They shake hands, snap their fingers.*)
The father of spinning tops who refused to have his
face turned by one little round of dance with the
drummer boys. The people of your house?

AKOTO : They are well, it is only Yamefo, that witch of a
woman who is determined to kill me. Do you know
what she did yesterday?

GOKU : Cooked for you with her hands she had put on the
earth?

AKOTO : No, that is not the only way they try to kill us.

GOKU : Hm, these women, they will be the death of us.
What did she do?

AKOTO : You know our last daughter Afizi. Afizi is
scarcely tall enough to sit on a kitchen stool without
her feet hanging in the air. Do you know what
Yamefo did yesterday? And I had warned her
several times; thrce markets ago I beat her for the
same thing; but her ears are as thick as oil pots
from Kuli.

GOKU : What did she do?

AKOTO : She sent Afizi to fetch water from the new well.
That woman wants to kill that child; but over my
dead body, then my name is not Akoto.

GOKU : And?

3

AKOTO: Afizi went to the well. I had just come back from the farm and I said I would have a bath. Yamefo said there was no water and that Afizi had gone to fetch some. As if I knew, I asked her where, but the witch kept mute, lengthened her face like a crocodile's. Before I closed my mouth there was a big commotion and yelling approaching my house, and my heart stopped beating. And I called my great grandfather, Agorsor, he who rode the invisible air to battle and brought home six enemy heads. You should have seen the commotion that followed.

GOKU (*taking out some snuff*): Was she all right?

AKOTO: Hmmm. She came to no harm. Agorsor himself brought her home. Have some snuff. It is very good. I bought it from a mangu trader yesterday. There stood Afizi crying: I shouted to my grandmother and took her in my arms. She had gone to the well, and as she was trying to turn the bucket her feet were danglng in the air; a woman, Dziwu's wife, saw her and raised the alarm before people came and caught the child. And they say that the well is as deep as ten farm ropes. (*Calls out*) Tchaa; I called Yamefo three times. Yamefo! silence, Yamefo! silence, Yamefo o o o! The house was empty; the woman had vanished, and up till now I haven't seen her.

GOKU (*incredulous*): You mean the woman has run away from home. Akoto, how does a grown-up woman who has borne five children for her husband run away like that?

AKOTO: I tell you she has run away. If she hasn't, where is she then?

GOKU: They say when you start to beat her, one can hear the sound of the blows at Agote. Did you report to the waterpolis people?

4

AKOTO (*shrugging*): No; not me. The last time I beat her
she ran into their sabitela on the road. You know
him, the big fat one with buttocks like a woman.
She told him the story. The fat fool sent for me to
the station. Do you know what he said, eh, Goku,
the flatulent ass said he will cane me? Have you
heard anything like this before? I, Akoto, of Agorsor's
heroic line, to have my buttocks beaten by an
uncircumcised dog-eater from Suponi because of a
woman!

GOKU (*with interest*): What did you do?

AKOTO (*angrily*): I turned round and spat on the floor. And
I told him, 'You don't know; you were our slaves, and
we sold your grandfather! I turned round to go.
He barked an order to a tall Kabre man from inside
and said something to him in Suponi. Then I knew
he had asked the man to beat me. He was playing
with fire. I, Akoto, of the calabash plant that has
rolled from long ago, I looked at the ceiling and I
called my ancestors, and said to them, 'When you
are alive, we do not suffer shame, not at the
hands of the offspring of slaves! The man came near
and spoke the whiteman's language through a
mouth that was black with kola and tobacco. Before
he was aware, I did not know where the strength
came from, I had thrown him in a gidigbo, and he
landed on his backside in the courtyard.

GOKU (*admiringly*): Eh, the son of a man; give me hand.
(*They shake hands and snap their fingers.*)

AKOTO: The sabitela stood there, staring like a man who
has lost his way to his own farm. I spat on the floor
again, took my cloth from the floor and burst into
my fetish song. I walked out of the station, and came
home.

GOKU: That's right. You are the offspring of Agorsor indeed. So where can Yamefo have gone to? Have you sent word to her people.

AKOTO: No; that uncle of hers is another. When Yamefo went and delivered Afizi, and refused to come back to me, I sent people. I even sent drinks, and gunpowder because I owed some funeral dues to that family. I did all this so that my wife could come back to my house. But that uncle of hers! that good-for-nothing snatcher of other people's wives, he opened his mouth wide and said he had heard I beat his niece, and that if I was a man I should come and take her myself. This is the message he sent to me, Akoto. When his nephew was fined in court in this town for smuggling and brewing local gin, who put out the money to get him out of prison? I will not stand here and see my wife's brother go to the government. I, Akoto, put out the money. When their granduncle, the one who sold medicine, came and died in the market place in this town, after an attack of hernia, who collected his body and brought it to my house, and sent word to them? But he has forgotten. Yes, the wielder of the knife forgets, but he who bears the scars never forgets. I have never done them any good deed in their lives. So he sends me that message.

GOKU: Eh, is he not afraid? Some people can be foolish. What happened?

AKOTO: When the messenger finished his message, I gave him a glass of gin, and asked him to go back to my wife's uncle, and say to him, 'The battle is far away beyond the lagoon, and you are dancing the war dance here among women'.

GOKU: That is the voice of the son of a man.

AKOTO: The messenger left. The next morning I got up, washed my face, and opened the ancestral hut. Dziwu and Kofiga, I had called to witness. Eh, the fires were sitting down quiet and burning. Then I spoke. I told them of the insult, the indignities, and the disgrace I have suffered from my wife's people. I was going to Asiyo to ask the meaning of the message. I poured them an offering. Did they accept? It branched off in seven places like the tributaries of the Mono. And I knew they have blessed. Then I took my matchet, and I set off. Dziwu and Kofiga wanted to come with me, but I said never; when war comes upon a man he must fight it alone. The community's war is a different matter. A man doesn't go asking his friends to fight for him.

GOKU: That is true; ehe, the son of a man!

AKOTO: I crossed the frontier at about six when the night water was still on the plants of the earth. I was all alone on the path. The sun was late rising that morning. I said to myself, this journey is fraught with trouble. I paused on the forked road leading to Asiyo and I called my great grandfather Agorsor seven times by name. I said to him, 'If the fault lies with me, punish me; if it lies with my enemies and your enemies, fire your gun'. Like it was from nowhere, a sharp report from an unexpected thunder rent the sky three times in the east, three times in the west, and once, only once over the village of Asiyo. That one had the sound of the royal gun at a funeral, and it lit and smashed in echoes, several of them over the whole sky. Then I knew my ancestor had spoken. Eh, he the warrior, the rider of the invisible air, has spoken. I entered the village.

GOKU: Ehe, tell me what did you see?

7

AKOTO: The village shrine was on fire on the outskirts.
Children, women, and goats were running in every
direction. I saw a woman fleeing towards me. I
stopped her and asked what was the matter. Thunder
has struck Yamefo's grandfather's house. That is
right. Who were they to play with the offspring of
the air rider? When the ram is still alive, how can
the ewes perform weed? When I approached the
house, it was still burning. Yamefo's grandfather,
Dzide himself, had been struck down in the lightning
and that uncle of hers who had sent that empty
threat to me had his cloth burnt off his very bottom.
I took Yamefo's hand; she was crying. I put the
baby on her back, loaded her belongings on her
head and brought her to my house.

GOKU: Eh, the seeds of the giant gourd, the rolling uncon-
trollable owner of the piece of land on which he
squats. Give me hand.

AKOTO: That is my name! (*They shake hands and snap their
fingers.*)

GOKU: So where has Yamefo gone to? Eh, women, they
will be our destruction. That is why I can marry
only one wife.

AKOTO: That is not the point. A man who fills the
household with women is a vain man who thinks it is
manliness to surround himself with women who
bring other people's children into his home to call
him father. He is a fool. Manliness consists of what
medicine you have eaten; from which ancestors
you spring; and what you are going to leave behind to
your offspring. The sprat cannot beget the mackerel.

GOKU: Yes, it is true indeed what you say. Today it is
hard, having many wives I mean. What with all

these sharp book people passing through here,
surveyors and boy scouts capable of any mischief in
your bed. It is hard.

AKOTO: Yes, indeed. Look at Kofiga's second wife he
married from Pota; people returning from the
riverside caught her and that crook who calls himself doctor; the fellow who sells headache medicine.
Have you seen him here again? He has run away.
Kofiga has sworn to cut off his head.

GOKU: And is the woman still with him?

AKOTO: Yes, what can he do! If a child fouls your calf
with excrement you don't carve it off; you wash it
away with water. Anyway, I have told the leader
of the Asafo, the *warrior* boys, to help find Yamefo.
I will not beat her, but if they say she has run away
to her relatives again, I will not ask the ancestors
to intervene this time. I will use my own hand.

GOKU: Yes, yes, perhaps you can; but don't you think
these matters can be settled peacefully? Don't you
think you and Yamefo's family ought to sit over the
whole affair. You cannot go dragging in those who
went before to settle your quarrels and bring disaster
on the head of your enemies.

AKOTO (*disparagingly*): You are a woman; because you
spend the day slicing onions for your wives you have
forgotten what it is to be a man. Are you not the
descendant of the hippo himself? Did your ancestor
not lead a war wing against the Adas and bring
home enemy heads to adorn his drums? Did he and
my ancestor Agorsor not eat medicine together, and
perform great deeds for this land.

GOKU: Yes, yes, but another day has dawned, another . . .

9

AKOTO (*listening*): Listen to him, listen to the hippo's
offspring talking about another day, talking as if he
is wearing women's menstrual pads and performing
puberty rites. The ancestors are here. You can hear
them in the wind, in the trees, in the rivers, in the
air, in the storm that blows over our heads. Why do
you think they are with us? Just to watch us dance
the dance of women, and forget the bravery of men,
the strong heart of lions, the valour of the heroes that
conquered this land for us? And if our enemies
rebuff us with abuses, and heap disgrace upon our
heads, shall we forget from which tree we have
descended, from which loins we were delivered, and
embrace our enemies like cowards, and give them
drink and break kola with them? (*emphatically*) No.
No. For if we do so, the ancestors will turn their
guns on us and smite us down as the ungrateful
offspring who betrayed their manhood, who betrayed
their names. They will smite us down at the
first cock for we are not men. We are women,
chattering in the market place while our fathers are
being insulted by the descendants of thieves, cowards
and slaves. Let Yamefo's uncle offer me challenge
again, and we will see what is in the skies, then I
am not Agorsor's descendant.

GOKU (*looking into the distance and pointing*): There are some
people coming. It looks like the sabitela, and about
six waterpolis.

AKOTO (*looking in the same direction*): Yes, indeed, it's them.
(*hurriedly*) Ah, Goku, I must go now; greet your
household for me.

POLICE CONSTABLE (*calling out*): Big man, big man,
stop. (*approaching*) Are you Akoto, the husband of
Yamefo of the village of Asigo?

AKOTO: Yes, that is me. But you know me; he who stays in his shell and gives trouble to onlookers.

POLICE CONSTABLE: You are under arrest . . . (*taking out handcuffs*) for arson, assault and battery, and conduct prejudicial to the breach of the peace.

AKOTO: Eh? What did you say? Me? Under arrest? For what? Let me alone. You hear? I? The offspring of Agorsor, the rider of invisible air to battle, the one who brought home from battle six enemy heads, and speaks through the voice of thunder. Ah, look at these offspring of dog-eaters eh, the grandchildren of slaves, the children of slave concubines.

POLICE CONSTABLE: You shut your mouth. When you go to the magistrate you go and say your say.

AKOTO: But one minute, I have taken purgative; I drank it this morning. Please.

POLICE CONSTABLE: When you go before the magistrate tell him then that you have taken purgative.

AKOTO: Eh, is this me, the offspring of Agorsor, the rider of the air the spirit of fire that speaks through the voice of thunder . . . (*His voice fades as he is dragged away*).

CURTAIN

The Magic Pool

KULDIP SONDHI

Kuldip Sondhi *was born in Lahore in 1924, and went to school in Kenya after his family had gone there to settle. Later he took an M.Sc. in Aeronautical Engineering in U.S.A. He has always written as a hobby. Another play,* Undesignated *has been published in* Short East African Plays *(AWS 28) and* With Strings *and* Encounter *were published in Cosmo Pieterse's selection of* Ten One Act Plays *(AWS 34). He works in Mombasa.*

CHARACTERS

City-Boy, a *youth from town/city*
James, *gang leader*
Girl
3rd Boy
2 Other Girls
Chengo, *hunchbacked boy*
Girl-Spirit

} *Five village youths*

The Magic Pool

The Stage is divided into two parts by a sloping line of trees. In the right half there is a single tree. In the left half there is a pool surrounded by bushes and trees. The pool is dimly lit. The back curtain shows a road with a village on one side and coastal vegetation all round the road. The stage is lit to show the appropriate time of day – evening. A group of six youths – three boys and three girls – are gathered under the tree on the right side of the stage. The boys are dressed in narrow trousers and coloured shirts. The biggest among them, a quiet, cold type is the gang leader. He strums a guitar, leans against the tree. The second boy also dressed city wise – and called City-Boy – is twisting to the tune. He is partnered by a girl in a frock; of the three girls she is the only one in the play who speaks. The third boy dances with a village girl in Giriama skirt and beads. The third girl, also dressed in skirt and beads sits on the ground nodding and occasionally clapping her hands to the music. From the dividing line of trees a hunchbacked boy is watching the dancing. The girl in the frock nudges City-Boy as they dance and he sees the hunchback in the trees.

CITY-BOY (*twisting*): Look, James!

JAMES: Hmmmm?

GIRL (*in frock, tittering*): That is Chengo.

CITY-BOY: There, through those trees. (*pointing at hunchback watching them*)

JAMES: What?

CITY-BOY: A creature from the bush!

JAMES: We are in the bush.

GIRL: Everyone knows Chengo here.

CITY-BOY: Here!

15

GIRL: This is only a village, City-Boy!

CITY-BOY: James man!

JAMES: Yes?

CITY-BOY: Just look man – a creature from the bush is watching us!

JAMES: Is he? (*glances sideways to see the hunchback boy come towards them*)

GIRL: He knows Chengo.

CITY-BOY: No! Do you know him, James?

JAMES: I was born here.

CITY-BOY: I was born in Mombasa.

GIRL: That is why you are called City-Boy.

CITY-BOY: I would die if I lived here – (*does a bushman's parody dance*) – oof!

GIRL: Mombasa is only 20 miles from this village, City-Boy.

CITY-BOY: Too far for me – look! (*Chengo comes out and walks towards them.*)

CHENGO: Jambo James.

JAMES: Jambo Chengo.

CHENGO: Jambo friends. I heard your music at the pool.

CITY-BOY: What pool?

CHENGO: There, through those trees. You can't see it from here.

JAMES: The same pool?

CHENGO: You remember it then?

JAMES: Of course. This village never changes.

CITY-BOY: What kind of pool is this?

JAMES: A special pool. It has water in it. (*Others laugh, City-Boy looks indignantly at them.*)

GIRL: He always sits there.

CITY-BOY: Doing what?

GIRL (*tittering*): No one knows.

JAMES: Still thinking, Chengo?

CHENGO: You know me!

CITY-BOY: Man, what a life! Sitting and thinking by a pool.

GIRL: He is known for that.

CITY-BOY (*surprised*): For sitting by a pool?

JAMES: No, for nothing.

CITY-BOY (*laughing*): Of course! (*stops twisting as James slows down beat*)

CHENGO: Are you staying long, James?

JAMES: No, we came in the morning and return on the evening bus, Chengo.

CITY-BOY: To live in this wilderness – Man, what a life!

CHENGO: I went to Mombasa once, but I didn't like it –

CITY-BOY: He didn't like the city! Did you hear that?

JAMES: Why didn't you like it, Chengo?

CHENGO: I tried to get work but no one would listen to me.

CITY-BOY: Did you talk to them about the pool? (*Girls titter.*)

17

CHENGO: No. But I was glad to return.

CITY-BOY: And I too shall be glad to return, let me tell you. God, what a place!

JAMES: It's hard to get work in the city, Chengo, but it's even harder to live out of it once it gets into your blood. (*strums guitar slowly, thoughtfully for a while*) Stay away from it, Chengo.

CHENGO: What work do you do there, James?

JAMES: This. I play in a bar.

GIRL: When he plays everyone sings and dances.

CITY-BOY: This one's never seen a bar. He sits by his pool.

CHENGO: Play again, James. I would like to listen.

CITY-BOY (*mimicking*): Play again, James. He wants to listen.
James plays again. City-Boy glances tauntingly at Chengo and, catching frocked girl, begins twisting. The third boy sits. Chengo makes a move to one of the girls. She turns aside. The third girl does the same. Gang leader smiles faintly and continues playing.

CITY-BOY: You couldn't do this, man. Look at you!

GIRL: He thinks a lot.

CITY-BOY: Of what? He wants to do a dance. But look at him! James, shall we go to his pool? Then he can think and dance all in one. Think and dance together. (*does a grotesque parody. Others laugh.*)

CHENGO: You talk a lot, my friend.

CITY-BOY: There are no pools in the city to talk about – my friend!

CHENGO: I am not your enemy.

JAMES: He is not your friend, Chengo.

CITY-BOY: This bushman?

CHENGO: You are no different to me. We are all alike.

CITY-BOY: All alike? (*stops twisting and looks at others in amazement*) Did you hear that?

JAMES (*smiles sardonically*): I heard.

CITY-BOY: No one is like you. You are – you are – I don't know what you are.

CHENGO: I am a man.

CITY-BOY: What a man! Go back to your pool, you creature!

JAMES: He is not your friend, Chengo.

CITY-BOY (*laughs*): His friend! If he came to the city, the girls would run screaming. Can you not see him in the traffic, bobbing and weaving like a camel? (*another cruel parody*) – You hunchback!

CHENGO: You are a bad man.

CITY-BOY: What!

JAMES: Leave him alone, City-Boy. It's time we went and got another drink. (*holds up empty bottle*) – I said leave him.

CITY-BOY: Yes, let's leave him. (*Girls titter, looking at Chengo who walks back through trees followed by City-Boy's laughter.*) Go back to your pool, you camel . . . you nyama!

Boys and girls all leave stage by right exit. Chengo walks to pool and sits by its edge. Its surface is faintly lit. He gazes distraught into its depths and speaks.

CHENGO : They hate me, they throw stones at me – why?
Because I am like this? (*walks round pool*) If I did
not feel, if I did not think, if I were really different
to them, if. . . . if I were dead? Yes, dead and free
from the sounds of their mocking laughter. Now!
(*draws knife*) Here, in these waters where I have
poured my sorrows, here . . . but why! Why? Only
because I have a hump – eh? No! Because I can see
into them. They hate me but they fear me too. Yes,
they fear me. Me – ha ha! And me . . . can I not
mock them in return, hate them and fight like they
do, shout abuse . . . call them liars and thieves . . . .
no, I cannot. I want their friendship . . . their love
. . . Oh God! A camel, a fool, a hunchback, yes, that
is what they said. And no girl looks at me without
shuddering. They are right. A hunchback, a camel.
Nyama! Die, you animal!

*He raises his knife for the fatal plunge. There is a blinding
flash across the pool. He falls in a stupor. His knife falls
and sinks into the pool. When the light clears a beautiful
Giriama girl is sitting beside him dangling her feet in the
water. She smiles at him. Recovered, he gazes at her in
astonishment.*

CHENGO : Who are you?

GIRL-SPIRIT : The Spirit of the pool.

CHENGO : The Spirit of the pool?

GIRL-SPIRIT : Yes, you called me and I came.

CHENGO : But how? Are you real?

GIRL-SPIRIT : Real in the realm where fantasies unfold,
Grown bright o'er this starlit forest pool.
I come, wondrous boy, not from heaven or hell,
But from deep within these very waters,
Woken by your longings that weave a spell.

The spirit of the pool you summoned,
Chengo, behold, that is me!

CHENGO (*looks at her, then turns to look at himself in the pool*):
Then I am not dead or dreaming. No, how could I
be . . . that's me! (*turns to Spirit*)
But tell me more, Spirit. Speak!

GIRL-SPIRIT: Speak? Yes, then speak I shall, so listen
Boy:
Life breathes in every leaf and drop of rain,
Hides in every laugh and twinge of pain,
Courses through all the veins of Existence.
Yet mortals blind, except they feel and see,
Disbelieve the universe sometimes glimpsed,
Gone, before it can be grasped or seen,
In all the hollow sounds of daily strife;
Disbelieve that, in caverns of the Spirit,
Treasures sparkle in vast multitudes
Guarded o'er by the five slave senses.
Yet perchance the mind stumble through this door.
It risks the visions of Revelation
In the galaxies surging at its Core:
Where Life wings free on timeless, golden plains
And sunrise and sunsets blaze as One,
Where, expunged of Hate and Ignorance,
The Truth in all full majesty unfolds
A wisdom undefinable and supreme.

CHENGO: What words! And . . . you'll be my friend, you
won't laugh at me?

GIRL-SPIRIT (*smiling*): Laugh . . . at you?

CHENGO (*eager*): Then you will appear when I call you?

GIRL-SPIRIT: First, sieve pride and petulance through the
net

And cool the sudden heat of blind encounters
If fluttering, sharp with the pain of deprivation,
And poisoned arrows falling, thickly wound,
Draw out those barbs, equally to quench its flaring
    hatreds.
If wicked storms froth in mad-dog mouths,
Let not your own crackle lightning in return,
Or bestial echoes, drummed skullwards, must roam,
Despoiling, through green valleys of the mind.
But trapped, on some lonely crumpling peak
With cities of sin hell-glittering on swamps below,
Then shout! And in the whirling drop I will appear!
The call that makes for my creation
Must have that kind of inspiration.

CHENGO: I promise, Spirit! (*holds out hands as spirit vanishes. He gazes at the empty pool in astonishment and from the right entrance James and his gang return drinking beer from bottles.*)

JAMES (*casting aside cigarette*): To live in this wilderness is to live as fools. No lights, no money, no fun, nothing.

CITY-BOY: How true! (*nods to skirted girls*) These people live like animals.

GIRLS (*dismayed*): Ehh!

CITY-BOY: What do you people do in the bush? The comforts of the city are unknown here.

JAMES: And your brains though city-skilled are empty as any bush-born fool's!
    (*Girls titter*)

CITY-BOY: I only meant —

JAMES: I know what you meant.
    Chengo turns at the pool and starts walking towards the gang.

CITY-BOY: But —

JAMES: Yes?

CITY-BOY: Nothing.

GIRL: Look, here comes Chengo.

CITY-BOY: Again!

JAMES: He is strange, that man.

CITY-BOY: He is not a man.

JAMES: You don't understand Chengo.

CITY-BOY: Who does! I swear James, look at him, laughing like a camel as he comes!

JAMES: Perhaps he's found a woman.

GIRL: What woman could he find?

JAMES: Who knows, let him come.

CHENGO: Jambo James.

JAMES: Jambo Chengo.

CHENGO: Jambo friends.

GIRL: Have you come from the pool, Chengo?

CHENGO: Yes.

CITY-BOY (*disgusted*): Always his pool. Is it a magic pool?

CHENGO: Yes! A magic pool! (*laughs happily*)

CITY-BOY: The man's mad!

JAMES: Have you found something, Chengo?

CHENGO: I found a friend.

CITY-BOY (*to others*): He found a friend. A wonderful friend.

CHENGO: That's right. A beautiful, wonderful friend!

JAMES: Is it a woman Chengo?

CITY-BOY: The woman of the pool!

CHENGO: Yes, yes, the woman of the pool!

CITY-BOY: Why, the man is mad.

JAMES: Tell me, Chengo, how did you find her, this woman?

CHENGO (*glancing at them in suspicion*): I can't tell you any more. (*At this James smiles, City-Boy bursts out laughing.*)

CHENGO (*indignant*): But it's true, true I say.

CITY-BOY: Your pool is true. (*points*) That we know.

CHENGO: The woman too.

JAMES: Then where is she?
(*Silence all round. They all look at Chengo. He looks back at them desperately, knowing himself trapped.*)

CHENGO: She has returned.

CITY-BOY: Into the pool?

CHENGO: Yes! (*Loud laughter from others, except James.*)

JAMES: Go and sit by your pool, Chengo. (*Twangs guitar in dismissal.*)

CHENGO: But she lives. I swear she does.

CITY-BOY: For you?

CHENGO: Yes. For me, only for me!

CITY-BOY: And is she like you, humped like a camel?

CHENGO: She is beautiful, beautiful I say —

CITY-BOY: Then let's see her.
(*Chengo is silent.*)

24

The Magic Pool

JAMES (*softly*): Chengo, if she lives, can't she come before us? We would like to see her.

CITY-BOY: James man, just look at him! If she lives, then these are spirits! (*pointing at girls beside him*)

GIRL (*tittering*): Who is your girl, Chengo? Does she live in this village?

CITY-BOY: Stupid, she lives in a pool! Is she a fish, Chengo – a she-fish?

JAMES: Bring her here, Chengo.

CHENGO (*furious*): You are all fools. You understand nothing.

CITY-BOY (*jumping up*): What! Did you hear that, James? This hunchback —

JAMES (*strumming*): Chengo, bring your girl or leave us.

CITY-BOY: Go and wait for her by your pool. Go!

CHENGO: She lives . . . she lives! (*runs off stage at right*)

JAMES: Something has come over him. I don't always understand that man. (*drains beer and sits at foot of tree, cradling his guitar*)

CITY-BOY: What's there to understand. He isn't a man (*pulls frocked girl by the hand*) – like me. Come, let's go. We waste time talking about that creature.

JAMES: Yes go . . . go, all of you. I've drunk too much. (*dismisses last village girl with a nod*) Go with them. I want to sleep. . . . this is a strange day . . . I don't know . . . something . . . strange (*strums guitar for a while, nods and falls asleep. Others leave. Night sounds from pool*).

Chengo returns through left entrance, goes to edge of pool and looks searchingly into it, shaking his head and walking round it as he speaks.

CHENGO: They say you do not live . . . you who talked to me. They will not believe me. How can they? They believe nothing . . . nothing! And yet, there you are . . . somewhere in there, a spirit who is also a woman. Woman appear – (*pause*) appear I say! No, I made a promise. I said I would not call unless I needed you. But now . . . I do need you! I would have them believe, I would show you to them. And you are there! No, no, I will not call again. They'll hear me and laugh. But I know you are there . . . only for me . . . Woman appear! (*becomes quiet as City-Boy and his girl return through right entrance. City-Boy wakes James*).

CITY-BOY: James, it's late. We'll miss the bus.

JAMES (*waking*): Yes . . . yes, let's go. I dreamed . . . no, never mind. (*shakes head*) God – let's leave this place.

CITY-BOY: Let's have a last drink before we go. It's a long drive back.

JAMES: All right . . . but I wish we hadn't come here today. (*Frocked girl nudges City-Boy seeing Chengo appear through the trees.*)

CITY-BOY: Oh, not him again!

GIRL (*tittering*): Where is his girl?

CITY-BOY: Yes, where is your girl?

CHENGO (*coolly*): I was only passing by.

CITY-BOY: Is she in the pool?

GIRL: How could she be in the pool? We are the only girls in the village who know how to swim.

CITY-BOY: Then she's been drowned.

CHENGO: Enough!

JAMES: Still without your friend, Chengo?

CITY-BOY (*talking fast and tauntingly*): She lives in the pool.

GIRL: She lives in the bush.

CITY-BOY: She lives in a tree.

GIRL: She lives in a stone.

CITY-BOY: She lives in the sea.

GIRL: She lives not at all!

CITY-BOY (*lying on his back and flapping his arms*): She lives, I say, she lives!

CHENGO: You are a dirty, filthy fool.

CITY-BOY: You lying camel, I'll break your face . . .

JAMES (*stopping City-Boy with his hand*): Chengo, go in peace, and leave us, to your simple pleasures.

CITY-BOY: If he calls me a fool again . . .

JAMES: Chengo, go! We are fools but we have our women. Now go, go before there is trouble.

CITY-BOY: I'm going to fight him.

JAMES: Sit.

CITY-BOY: But James . . .

JAMES (*lays aside guitar without looking up*): I said sit.

CITY-BOY (*sits, then jumps up again*): Go, you ugly brute – get out! (*Girl titters and whispers in his ear.*)

CITY-BOY (*shouts after the retreating Chengo*): Your woman is a WHORE. (*laughs breathlessly*) A whore, Chengo. (*Chengo stands stunned, whirls, charges*) He comes! (*Everyone leaps to their feet. There is a fight. The gang leader and City-Boy throw Chengo down.*)

CITY-BOY: James, the animal's down, I'll kill him.

JAMES: No!

CITY-BOY: Yes!
In a trice City-Boy has drawn out his snap-knife and stabbed Chengo on the ground. The others flee. James, now sober, stares aghast at what has happened.

JAMES: Oh no!

CITY-BOY (*breathing*): He's finished?

JAMES: So are we. Do you know what you have done?

CITY-BOY: He called me a fool.

JAMES: You are a fool. The police will be here soon. Look what you've done!

CITY-BOY: He attacked me.

JAMES: You'll hang.

CITY-BOY (*Looks scared*): Hang . . . hang? My God . . . No . . . no! (*runs off stage*)

JAMES (*muttering and shaking his head*): What have we done –

CHENGO (*groaning*): Ahhhh!

JAMES (*bending and touching Chengo*): Chengo . . . Chengo, talk to me. Say something.

CHENGO (*struggles fitfully to rise on his elbow, finally succeeds and looks at James*): Help me, James.

JAMES (*bending to hear him*): I am here, Chengo.

CHENGO: Take . . . take me to the pool.

JAMES: No!

CHENGO: To the pool, James.

JAMES: No, you must stay here. I'll get some help. You'll soon be all right, promise, you will —

CHENGO: Take me to the pool, James.

JAMES: No, Chengo!

CHENGO: Please, James.

JAMES: All right . . . all right, I'll take you there.
With his guitar slung across his shoulder he helps Chengo to the pool. It is now dark. Birds and frogs are calling between the trees. James looks about him with frightened eyes and lays Chengo down by the side of the pool.

CHENGO: She is here.

JAMES: Who?

CHENGO: The spirit of the pool.

JAMES: No . . . no! (*Looking about him, now thoroughly frightened. A bird screams in the tree behind him.*) God help you, Chengo. (*takes to his heels*)

CHENGO (*gasping*): It was my fault. I called her and she punished me. So be it. But now, how clear my vision grows: it was my love they feared, the love of the deformed . . . giving, never taking, alone like the trees, where storm and darkness gather deeper than the night. Forgive me, Oh spirit, for my pride, and forgive them too. They who so feared me that I have to die . . . but wait, beyond the roaring I hear whispers. There is a sinking and some lightness too . . . ah, I have one last request: Oh spirit of the pool, come to me once more, appear now!
Chengo rises on his elbow in a last effort, gasps and falls back. There is silence except for his breathing. Then there is a flash across the pool and the Spirit materializes by his side. She puts his head in her lap.

29

GIRL-SPIRIT: Thus summon'd wondrous Boy, I come, but
  alas,
  Our sorrows, winging high in stricken brilliance,
  Flash quivering shadows through earth's blind
    greenness,
  And in silence, swoop over this darkening pool.
  Yet from my grief rises a joy supreme,
  Knowing you have gained man's greatest wisdom:
  That there is in life an inviolate reason
  And, in forgiveness, heaven's most royal estate.
  Know it then, amid the warring of the Senses,
  That the soul, once freed, wanders not into
    oblivion,
  But soars untarnished into rejuvenation,
  Filled with the knowledge of man's salvation.
  Farewell sweet Boy.
  *Chengo takes last breath, rises, smiles and sinks in fading
  light over pool.*

CURTAIN

God's Deputy

SANYA DOSUNMU

Sanya Dosunmu *was born in the Western State of Nigeria. He was educated in Ibadan, a contemporary of the Nigerian musician, composer, and musicologist, Akin Euba, with whom the present play was first conceived as an opera. After studies and theatre work in Nigeria, Dosunmu spent some years in London, where he continued his studies and career in the theatre, taking part in productions at the Hampstead Theatre and the Royal Court Theatre. He returned to Nigeria in 1966 to be a director and later producer in the drama department of Nigerian Television; he is now Head of Drama in English with the Nigerian Broadcasting Corporation (T.V.). Music for* God's Deputy *has now been composed by Ayo Bankole – Senior Research Fellow in the Dept. of African Studies, University of Lagos.*

31

CHARACTERS

King, *a descendant of Gahmororo*
Otun Ajagajigi
Osi Ajagajigi } *his two chief counsellors*
Bashorun, *a chief in Western Nigeria*
Kori, *the king's wife*
Lape, *the king's sister*
Derin
Aweni } *two daughters of Bashorun*
Ogunmodede, *leader of the hunters*
7 hunters
Amope
Joke
Abeni } *girls*
Alake
Peju
Messengers and Attendants
Chorus of Subjects

SCENE ONE

The Scene is the Pavilion at the Gahmororo Palace in Western Nigeria. The set comprises the throne on a raised platform centrally situated up-stage. A horseshoe-shaped arch-corridor adjoins the raised platform at both sides. A large door stands directly behind the throne. Half-way through the first quarter-circle to the left of the platform a long archway leads to the other parts of the Palace. There are two stools, large and small, placed side by side at left mid-stage. A horsetail for the King, and a golden dagger conveniently displayed on the raised platform. The time is nine o'clock in the morning. It is an occasion marking the end of the Egungun (masquerade) festival. Time, late nineteenth century.

When the curtain rises, we find a crowd of people gathered at the Pavilion, and a few more people coming in and paying homage to the vacant throne. Messengers respond to the homages on behalf of the absent king, who later appears, dressed in full traditional garment, from the large door directly behind the throne. His behaviour is gay though dignified, and with an air of full authority. As he enters, the crowd hails him – men prostrating and women stooping in the traditional Yoruba fashion.

CROWD: Kabiyesi, kabiyesi!

MESSENGERS: Oba nki o.

> *The KING waves his white horsetail at the people as his attendants acknowledge their salutations. Music starts from the moment the king enters. He stops a little before the throne to acknowledge the cheers, and does not sit until after his speech following the chorus.*

OTUN: Kabiyesi, our king, great son of Gah.
> King, who gives the order
> For us all to obey.
> Next in rank to the god,

33

Son of Gah, respected king.
The day you came into the World
There was a velvet bed prepared for you.
There was gold,
There was money —
There were servants male and female;
There were maids to sing the lullaby
When your highness cried the yen-yen.

CHORUS: Kabiyesi our king, great son of Gah.
King who gives the order
For us all to obey.
Next in rank to the God,
Son of Gah, respected king,
Son of Gah, God's own deputy.

OSI: Our greatest symbol of authority,
True to fact, you are the God's deputy.
Son of Gah, God save you,
Long may you reign,
Long on your head may the crown remain,
Long on your feet the shoe.
We are thankful to God for your life,
May God accept our thanks.

CHORUS: Son of Gah, God save you,
Long may you reign,
Long on your head may the crown remain,
Long on your feet the shoe.
We are thankful to God for your life;
May God accept our thanks.

KING: Thank you, thank you all
Our loyal chiefs, thank you!
Thank you, thank you all
Loyal subjects, thank you!
We esteem your love and devotion. Thank you, thank
you all. (*pauses for speech*) It is our great . . . (*pauses*

while DERIN, *entering from left entrance up-stage, occupies
her place at right mid-stage as principal female Palace
singer*) . . . it is our great pleasure to welcome you
all, and to offer to you our special salutations on this
historic Egungun festival. (*sits on the throne*)

DERIN: Our great symbol of authority.
    True to fact you are God's deputy;
    You wear a crown of gold
    on your head;
    With your hand a beaded stick you hold.
    We are your slaves,
    We are your servants.
    May there be peace at your time,
    May we be blessed at your time,
    May we bear children male and female.
    We wish you joy.
    Long may you reign,
    Long on thy head —

KING: Bless you maiden . . . it is our personal hope that
    all your wishes come true. (*sighs*) Sometimes we . . .
    we feel, no, you make us feel as if the whole . . . the
    whole wide world is under our feet—

DERIN: Son of Gah, not only the whole world,
    But all the people in it! Kabiyesi.

KING (*spiritedly*): You wake up our dormant spirit to a
    higher plane with your sweet tongue. But we have
    no ambition beyond having yourself alone under our
    feet . . . (*There is dead silence from all quarters.*)

BASHORUN: Great king, you are indeed a symbol of
    authority, next in rank to the God. But I do not
    approve of my daughter being under your feet . . .
    My daughter is already – my lord, she has been
    promised in marriage to the son of my fellow chief—

KING : You may well cancel your allegiance to this fellow chief of yours – because we intend to make her our eyes. She will know our every movement; she will know our coming in and our going out. She will bear us princes and princesses. We decide to place her under our feet, and hereby declare —

BASHORUN : You shall not declare anything, good great king, I shall not give it my blessing . . . (*moves as if in pain, then bursts into passionate singing*)
To thee king, is my honour due.
Honour is due to the forest,
The hare does give it.
Honour is due to the grassland;
If the deer fails to honour the forest
Or the hare the grassland,
Then they get trapped!
King, great king, I have always honoured thee;
Given to thee all my love and devotion,
Yet I get trapped;
Trapped between your desire for my daughter
And her earlier betrothal to the son of a friend!
No, king, I cannot give my blessing
This I can only do but once!
'Tis too late, king,
Declare not my daughter your wife.

KING (*firmly but calmly*) : All the same we shall have our object. We hereby declare her a wife to ourselves and wish to entertain no more questions on that subject. She has spent her last day in your house; henceforth, she shall remain in our palace house.

BASHORUN : May it please your —

KING : Nothing shall please us more . . . (*turns his back to Bashorun, and almost immediately faces him again, still firmly*) Nothing . . . we have set our foot on her and shall not retrace our step. (BASHORUN *walks out*

*in annoyance and his daughter sobs. After a short pause
the* KING *speaks*) I see; your father, our once loyal
Bashorun, now plots against our marrying his
daughter. How treacherous! Well, he must explain
this at a later date. Meanwhile —

DERIN (*fearfully*): No, no, no, good great king. My father
is not against you . . . I shall go and call him back!
My father is not against your highness.

KING (*holding her back*): Not now damsel —
Call him not.
We shall first hold counsel
To find out his plot.
(*sharp music stops abruptly, and the* KING *brightens up*)

KING: Oh, dear loyal subjects, we have almost forgotten
this is a festive occasion. We ought to be happy
because we are all hale and hearty. We, on our part,
shall not permit a thing as little as courtship to mar
the happiness of our subjects.
*Now there can be heard the sound of distant drumming and
of a bell* (agogo). *A messenger enters, pays due homage to
the king and announces the arrival of the masquerade.*

MESSENGER: The mask, kabiyesi, is come.

KING: Ask him and his fellows in. (*turning to his subjects*)
You must all feel gay and merry. (*walks around
gaily waving his horsetail at them, and then walks towards
his throne*) We shall ourselves sit on the throne of
our fathers to watch the mask dance to pleasure
us all.
*As the king resumes his seat, there is a joint cheer of
'Kabiyesi' from all the subjects. There is a short introduction
to the chorus which follows almost immediately.*

CHORUS: Kabiyesi our King, great son of Gah,
King who gives the order

For us all to obey.
You are next in rank to the God,
Son of Gah, respected King;
Son of Gah, God's deputy.
We love thee, and praise thee,
And wish thee, son of Gah,
Long to reign over us,
Ase, may it be so.
(*Enter the mask and his followers.*)

FOLLOWERS: Mask of Olufakun,
God of Olufakun,
Joy of Olufakun,
Pride of Olufakun . . .
(*This music is repeated three times with the mask and his
brother dancing round the stage. See notes which follow the
play on the mask's entrance. Then the king rises to deliver
his festival speech*).

KING (*making gestures for silence*): This, no doubt, is another
successful celebration of the Egungun festival. We
are all very pleased with the dance of the mask and
his brother, and with the music of his followers.
May you all be here next year for this same
celebration! May you all be blessed with healthy
children! May your body and soul taste of peaceful
existence during this new year! Your head will not
ache! Your liver will not ail you! I wish you abundance
of money and children both male and female. Death
will not overcome you! Long, long may you all
live.

*There are responses of 'Amin' and 'Ase', alternately, after
every wish the king makes.*
*Then follows the ritual ceremony between the mask and
king. (See notes at end of play on Rituals.) There are
cheers of 'Kabiyesi' from the subjects as the king finishes
the ritual and rises to dance with the mask; his followers,*

*and the chorus of subjects in succession dance away from
the stage. The king waves them good-bye with his horsetail.
But the Otun lingers behind, and as the music dies away
the King beckons to him.*

OTUN: Kabiyesi.

KING: What can we say has given Bashorun all that
boldness to question our authority? Who is this
Chief and friend of his and the young man in our
Kingdom to whom Derin has been betrothed?

OTUN: Kabiyesi. I can assure your highness that Bashorun
did not intend to question your authority. It is a
long story behind the betrothal of his beautiful
daughter whom your highness happens to be in
love with. It should be unpleasant to the ears of
your highness, so I plead with your highness not to
listen to it —

KING (*with rising temper*): Listen to it I shall, loyal Otun,
son of Adegbola, general of the army at war, and
their commander at peace. Your father was a brave
man, and was not my father a brave man too? Did
he not personally lead his army during the Dahomey
wars? Did he not conquer all his enemies? Was he
not the only king who boldly, and bodily, collected
taxes from all his districts and enemies, and came
back to his throne alive? What? Did you say a mere
story would upset us? Nay, be it far from us . . .
Tell us, then, all about Derin.

OTUN: A snail dies if it tastes the salt!

KING: . . . tastes the salt!

OTUN: At the cry of Oro, women halt.

KING: . . . sure they halt.

OTUN: A butterfly which kicks against the thorns tears his skin!

KING: . . . tears his skin.

OTUN: Two hundred beasts with horns dare not look on the lion's skin!

KING AND OTUN: They dare not, dare not, dare not.

OTUN: Your highness, our fathers always sang that song to illustrate your father's bravery. But even they realized how little justice it did to him. He was a king amongst kings. A tall lanky handsome man with a beautiful set of teeth which women described in their songs as golden. You are an enlarged copy of your father's looks and bravery . . . Now then, your highness, listen while I tell you the story . . .

OTUN: There lived a rich woman once,
Married to the wealthy king of Ketu.
By her a blind boy was born
Which blind prince became Alaketu.
This rich woman was our kin,
Her grandson brave, his name Morakin,
He led an army 'gainst Morada
And so became our Bada.

KING: And so became our Bada.

OTUN: Our Bada he has a son,
Apple of his eye, his exact image.
He learnt books, and shone like sun
'Midst our unread sons of the village.
He works in Jos – so far away!
Money he has, in life finds his way
He loves Derin, told his father so,
Bada pays the dowry; so . . .

KING : So, we are in this conflict.
*Otun nods his head in confirmation of the King's conclusion.
There is a long silence between them, each expecting the
other to speak next.*

KING ⎱ *(together)* :   If —
OTUN ⎰   The —

KING *(indicating that Otun should go ahead)* : Well, well . . .

OTUN : Well, your highness, you can clearly see the diffi-
cult position in which Bashorun is, and in which you
yourself are, by creating this situation.

KING *(with confidence)* : Still, a king on his throne is a
symbol of authority and the God's own deputy.
While I occupy this throne of my father's, I shall
not fail to have what I desire in my kingdom. My
father never failed!

OTUN : Kabiyesi.

KING : Has the maiden been taken to my chamber as I
ordered?

OTUN : Kabiyesi.

KING : We shall ourselves knock at the door, and when
she comes out, we shall express our passion to her
and seek to know what she thinks of us. If it be
promising, we shall not give up the fight.

OTUN : The fight! Your highness needs not call it the fight;
your highness need only to command.
*The king knocks three times at the large door behind the
throne.*

DERIN *(from within)* : Who are you? I don't know you.
Tell me who you are, and what you want with
me. What do you want of me?

KING : Oh, my slim, lovely wife
    What makes you speak like this?
    Granted you know not the ocean,
    Don't you ever see the sky?
    And if you have never seen the lagoon
    Don't you taste salt in your soup?
    Ah, even if you don't know your love,
    Can't you recognise his voice?
    – Full of love:
    Tender passion, from the very citadel of his heart.
    My love, my wife, I know you too well:
    I know your pair of tender eyes too well,
    Your feet are adorned with crimson cream,
    Yes.
    Your skin, like an orange ripe, is fair . . . (*knocks*)
    Come out;
    Speak to me,
    To me, your love,
    Your only one,
    The key of your heart and soul.
    *There is no answer, he hesitates a little, then walks down
    to sum up courage in the following song.*

KING : The tortoise never has head-ache,
    The snail never has liver-ache
    The fish inside water never feels cold
    There is no hold for the bird in the sky!
    A man's inherited authority should not frighten him.
    *Brightly, and with determination the king walks back to the
    door and raps three times at it. He then walks to mid-stage
    where he stands.*

DERIN (*coming out*) : Here I am, King. I heard you knocking
    once.

KING : No, three times!

DERIN : Once . . . King.
    And as your loyal subject,
    I hastened here my King.

KING: No,
It is my lover,
And wife,
That hastened to be with me.

DERIN: If that soothes your highness, if it suits you
better;
But I cannot see a marriage yet:
My father's consent has not been given.

KING: Come (*holds her by the hand*), if your father gives his
blessing . . . will, will you marry us?

DERIN: Oh king, he has already given his blessing,
And as you will agree,
This he can do only but once! (*withdraws her hands
from his, and moves down stage*)

KING (*contemplating, then suddenly*): Well, maiden, we have
chosen you for our wife, and though there be need
to behead your father, our wife you shall remain.

OTUN: May that not be a necessity, your highness.
Kabiyesi, this maiden that you see is a chosen queen
from heaven – I can read that from her look and
gait. With a little patience, Kabiyesi, she will soon
be what you desire. (*to Derin*) I am sure you will not
regret it.

DERIN: Regret it or not, I cannot act against my father's
wish. I'd rather be beheaded too, because his death
shall only strengthen my decision.

KING: What! Do you take us so lightly? Well, we shall
first lay our hands on Bada – the man who claims
our queen for his son – he shall not live to see the
set of this sun. If then we fail in our bid, it shall be
his son next, and then your father, and . . . and any
one who stands between us and your heart. (*walks
out via the door behind his throne, banging the door hard
after him*)

OTUN: Well, daughter, you will not regret it. I am sure of
it. As to your father's stand, he may even have
changed his mind now. Besides, who knows what
tomorrow has in stock and in store for us? We are
only sure of our lives yesterday, not even today or
tomorrow.

DERIN: Father, you seem to hit at the point each time you
talk . . . But even if my father gives his consent, I
fear to climb so high lest I fall and break my
backbone! When a girl of my age and birth aims at
becoming a queen, she may live to regret it.

OTUN: Hm . . . as to that, you are right indeed. And you
are a wise girl too. But let me tell you a story about
Iyabo – a maiden who was in an identical position
some years ago. She was a wise girl too, and if you
follow her example, I am sure you will not regret it.
*Leading Derin to the stools, he sits on the big one while she
sits on the other.*

OTUN: A father had a daughter once,
Iyabo was her name
Her skin was fair, her legs were straight,
And bright she was indeed!

DERIN: And am I bright? How can you tell?
Can you tell if I am bright?

OTUN: From East and West and North and South
The rain of suitors fell.
She priced her breasts, her pointed breasts
And turned them all away!

DERIN: She's right I hope, but why?

OTUN: The suitors jaunty, bold and gay,
They brought her father gifts.
The girl she didn't like the men,
Returned their gifts to them!

44

DERIN: She acted wisely too . . .

OTUN: A king, we're told, he loved the girl.
He brought the dowry all!
The father tried, but all in vain,
To change his daughter's mind.

DERIN: He's wrong to think he could.

OTUN (*rising and moving towards centre lower stage*)
And Iyabo was right indeed
For choosing such a King. (*beckons to Derin*)
They lived together years and years
And never knew regret!

BOTH (*facing each other, Otun reassuring while Derin is
apprehensive*):
They never knew regret!

SCENE TWO

*Takes place in the compound of the Bashorun. The Set
comprises the back view of Bashorun's own house, and the
front view of three other, smaller houses. The corridor
passing through Bashorun's house is clearly visible. At the
end of it, near to the audience, can be seen a native stove
(adogan or aro) with boiling water on it. There are also
other cooking utensils around. The spaces between the
houses serve as entrances and exits. There is an Odan tree
in the centre of the compound with an iron staff typical
of the Ogun worshippers tied on to it, 12 cowries and a red
feather for the hieroglyphic messages. A wooden armchair
is placed very close to the wall left of Bashorun's house.
There are signs of life in all the houses. It is evening,
time: about nine p.m. There is bright moonlight.
The curtain rises and we see Kori — a middle-aged woman —
bringing a measure of yam flour to prepare her family's
supper. Her daughter, Aweni, sister to Derin, (she is
about eleven years old) most impatiently holds on to her*

45

*mother's wrapper, asking where her sister Derin has been
since morning.*

AWENI: Where is she, mother? Where is she?
Kori does not answer, instead she gently shakes her off.

AWENI: Mother . . . m-o-t-h-e-r.

KORI: Yes, darling, I have told you over and over again;
Derin has gone on an errand for me.

AWENI: Well . . . (*turns away frustrated, and sits in the doorway,
only to say after a while*) But you told me she would
be back for lunch, and she wasn't.

KORI (*taking water out of the bucket with a Calabash bowl*):
I am sorry about that . . . (*suddenly*) Oh, Aweni,
Aren't we unlucky?

AWENI: What is't mother?

KORI: Our food is not done, and I haven't a jot of extra
yam flour at home to make it good. Would you like
to go into the compound and sing for a loan of
flour, please?

AWENI: Yes, mother. (*hurries into the compound, and sitting on
the edge of the armchair, begins to sing*)
Amala 'ya mi ro,
  Kole Kole,
Amala 'ya mi ro,
  Kole kole,
Amala 'ya mi ro,
  Kole kole,
Amala 'ya mi ro,
  Kole kole.
*Amope and Alake enter from the left and right entrances
respectively as Aweni sings the last line, and they join in
the chorus.*

AWENI, AMOPE and ALAKE: Kole kole.

AWENI: Ah! It's you, Amope, (*turning right*) and you too, Alake. Has your mother any flour at home, Amope?

AMOPE: Yes, she has . . . (*she hops back into the house from which she came out, chanting repeatedly*) Yes she has, yes she has . . .

ALAKE (*sitting on the ground, and picking up some pebbles with which she toys*): I am sorry, Aweni, my mother travelled this morning and didn't leave her keys.

AWENI: Yes, I remember my mother told me auntie Lape has gone to call my sister home.

AMOPE (*re-appearing with a measure of yam flour, still chanting*): Yes she has, here it is.
She hands the flour to Aweni, and all three of them hop in to give the flour to Kori who has, in the meantime, continued with her cooking.

AWENI: Well, mother, here's some flour for you, we got it from Amope's mother . . . Mother . . . Mother . . .

KORI: Yes, darling.

AWENI: Can you make enough for me and my friends, please? . . . and for sister Derin and Amope's mother in case they come back and find us eating?

KORI: I shall, darling.

AWENI: Thank you, mother . . . mother, we shall go into the compound to play, please call us when you are ready.

KORI: It is not bad; I shall call you when I am ready.

AWENI: Thank you, mother. Don't forget Derin.
(*They all trot away and sit left mid-stage a little way before the Odan tree. At this instant Peju and Abeni arrive together, and later Joke arrives.*) We shall play 'Boko, boko'. (*Aweni turns left and sees Preju and Abeni arriving.*)

Here, hurry up and join in our play. (*She then discovers the other girl – Joke.*) Come along, Joke, we are ready . . . you go into hiding, we shall call on you when we are ready and if you recover the stone on your arrival, you shall marry the king. (*she picks up a stone*) Let us start now. Oya.

AWENI OTHERS } (*together*): Boko boko-o
Aluboko

AWENI: Bo boko nle

OTHERS: Aluboko

AWENI: Bo boko lodo

OTHERS: Aluboko

AWENI OTHERS } (*together*): Boko, boko-o
Aluboko

There is silence as Aweni calls on Joke to come out.

AWENI: You can come now. (*As Joke blunders at recovering the stone from the right target, they all giggle, but when she finally chooses a wrong target, they all laugh heartily. Aweni recovers the stone and gives it to Joke to have her choice.*) You can have now your chance on any of us—

JOKE (*anxiously seizing the stone from her*):
It's you, Aweni, I am choosing you to go and hide. If you recover the stone on your return you shall marry the king; if you can't, you shall (*gleefully*) m-a-r-r-y his s-e-r-v-a-n-t. (*They all laugh merrily at this playful suggestion.*) You may go now. (*Aweni hurries away and the game is repeated as before.*) All set now? Aweni, you may come out.

AWENI (*after a little consideration of the players, and a few faulty near-moves and the giggling of her mates, finally recovers the stone, saying, amidst the cheers of her friends*)
But I can't marry the king! I am only a small child.

ALAKE: All right, let's have another game . . . er . . . um
. . . 'The King's Order'.

AWENI: What is the Order?

ADUKE (*distinctly feigning the dignity of a king*): W-h-o-s-e
t-w-o k-n-e-e-s f-o-l-d f-i-r-s-t, s-h-a-l-l b-e m-y
w-i-f-e.

OTHERS (*cheeringly, but not quite uniformly*): Yes, let's have
it.
*The musical introduction to the song which follows starts
when the girls are saying, 'Yes, let's have it'. (For the
procedure see notes on Games at the end of the play.)*

ALL: Kini kan nja mi labi kere
O nde mi gere
Epo olojo
Iyamuyamu
Ka boko soro loju elepo
Korokoro
Owo tun ra
Ese obara
Obara ni kija
O le le o
Kayi ko
Oba ni o ka yi ko.
(*song is repeated, and it's Aweni whose two knees fold
first*)

ALAKE: Well, Aweni, it has fallen on you again.
I think you have to marry the king.

AWENI (*amidst the playful cheers of her friends*): Not me, not
me, I have told you I am only a child.

ALAKE: Then make a substitute.

AWENI (*after a little consideration, brightens up*): My sister,
Derin . . . She can marry the king when she comes
back.

KORI (*from the door, calling the girls*): Ready now, girls, come in for supper. (*As they race in, Bashorun appears from left entrance, looking worried and dejected. Kori discovers him when the last of the children has got in. Without talking, she too goes in but soon comes out to ask*): Do you wish to take your food out here?

BASHORUN (*already seated on the armchair, looking moody*): Yes.
Kori goes in and returns with a covered tray of food which she places on a stool in front of her husband. No word passes between them. Bashorun stares at an empty space restlessly. Kori goes in to bring water for washing his hands. She re-enters to discover her husband is gone. Puts the water near the food and looks about. The introduction to the song which follows begins at the moment Bashorun leaves his armchair and walks out. It is slow, dense and contemplative.

KORI: He is gone again! This is serious. (*begins to sing*)

What can a wife do
When her husband behaves like this?
What can a wife do
When he becomes so uncompromising?
Even his food he would not take . . .   5
How can we be at one
In his bid, so stupid,
To reject his highness' hand
Choosing the hand of a peasant
For Derin, his daughter and mine?   10

Our World is invested
With choosing from the best;
There is nothing wrong with it!
My husband should be wise,
And not play the game of fools   15

50

By choosing from the worst.
Whoever rejects the velvet,
And uses a rag in its stead?
How can we be at one
In his bid, so stupid,
To reject his highness' hand;
Choosing the hand of a peasant
For Derin, his daughter and mine?

She turns her back to the audience, obviously frustrated by her husband's behaviour.

OTUN (*who has entered unnoticed on the twenty-third line of Kori's song, and is now joined by Osi and Lape, sings*):
Good evening, woman.

OSI
LAPE } (*together*): Good evening.

KORI (*turning to discover them*): Good evening all, and how are you? How are you, Lape? What happens to my child? Did you see her?

OTUN: Your daughter is well.

OSI: She sends you greetings.

LAPE: She is hale and hearty, but not very happy!

KORI: I don't expect! The king, I hear, has learnt that her dowry had been paid.

OTUN: Yes indeed . . . and she is willing —

KORI (*excitedly*): Willing what?

OTUN: To marry the king.

KORI: Well, but her father,
We cannot be at one
In his bid, so stupid,
To reject his highness' hand
Choosing the hand of a peasant
For Derin, his daughter and mine.

OTUN : Your husband may seem stupid to you, but he
has his reasons – a wise and upright fellow, poor
Bashorun – he has built for himself a name which
he would defend against all odds. He knows better
than you in this: and would not keep his name after
the fashion of Esu, cunning god who causes confusion.
(*Otun then sings the following song.*)

Song

Esu elegbara
Cunning god who causes confusion;
He made a bride, newly wed,
Steal a penny from a dame.
Excusing herself, the bride had said
'A penny is not worth much!'
But Esu knows much better:
That he has to keep his name;
And so he says of himself,
'If a big goat gets lost
Do not ask me;
If a fat sheep gets lost
Do not ask me.
If a cock gets lost
Which has crowed for years
Two and one
Do not ask me,
I never steal animals
I never steal birds
But,' Esu elegbara sighs,
'If you miss a dog, a black dog,
You may ask me:
There are sixty-one loaves at hand —
I eat twenty hot!
I eat thirty dry!
The other eleven – well,
That's what I use the dog's meat for!'

(*They all laugh at this, and Otun concludes*) You see that Esu finds a way out of the awful situation because even he will not mar his reputation!

KORI: Ha, ha, ha, you beat me with your philosophy.

LAPE: Otun is known for that.

OSI: There's truth in what he says. Your husband has his good name to keep.

OTUN: Your husband is different, he does not steal anything. He allays confusion by refusing the king, and standing by a friend who thought his own son would marry your daughter —

KORI: What? I can't understand you. Is he not going to marry her any more?

OSI: Listen, I have news for you and your husband.

KORI: What news? Good or bad?

OSI: Either, or it could be both, depending on how you take it.

BASHORUN (*who has entered unnoticed*): Break your news . . . (*discovers Lape*) Ah, wait a minute, here is my sister. (*to Lape*) Where is my daughter? I taught you how to bring her out!

LAPE: I regret that as she has been locked up in the inner chamber of the Palace, it was impossible for me to bring her out.

BASHORUN (*surprised*): Locked up?

LAPE: Yes.

BASHORUN: Well . . . Well . . . (*turning to Osi*) What news have you got?

OSI: 'Tis about our brave old Morakin, the captain of our army against the rebellious Morada.

53

BASHORUN: Our same old Bada, Bale of Ketu.

OSI: Hm, hm.

BASHORUN: His son is to marry my daughter.
He is an associate, and a good old friend.

OTUN: No doubt . . . we all grew up together.

OSI: He is dead!

LAPE ⎱ (*Severally*): What?
KORI ⎰ Dead!

BASHORUN (*sobs*): . . . That is too sad. Has his son learnt
of this great loss, and is he back from Jos? His
mother left home when he was a child of only two
years. Poor young boy.

OSI: She is back home too, though unaware of her
husband's death till she arrived.

KORI: What brought her home then?

OSI: According to her, she learnt that her son was going
to marry your daughter and has hurried home to
stop the marriage!

KORI: Has she any reason for it?

OSI: Yes, her reason is that you and she are cousins on
your mother's side. Your children cannot marry!

OTUN: Her mother was the fourth daughter of Bolaji, the
popular cloth dealer, who, I have since learnt, was
your grandmother.

KORI: Y-e-s . . . (*recollecting*) Yes, indeed!

AWENI (*entering and going to Kori*): Mother, there are two
men outside waiting to see my papa.

BASHORUN: Tell them to come in.
Aweni hurries out, returning with the two men.

54

1ST MAN: Good evening to you all in this compound.

2ND MAN: And peace.

BASHORUN: Good evening, what do you wish to see me about?

2ND MAN: To give you this . . . from our Bale, the new Alaketu (*hands over the hieroglyphic message to Bashorun. (See notes on messages at end of play.*)

BASHORUN (*passing the message in turn to Otun*): You interpret this to us.

OTUN (*considering the message*): It can only come from a relation. (*to Osi*) Do you note the red feather? . . . Blood relationship. Well, listen to the message:- (*translating*) By this set of six cowries I do draw you to myself and wish you draw closely to me. As by this feather I can only reach your ears, so I am expecting you to come to me, that is, I am hoping to see you immediately.

BASHORUN: Thank you . . . (*to Aweni*) Take your visitors in and give them water. We shall be with you immediately. (*Aweni and the men go into Bashorun's house.*) . . . Well . . . I shall reply to him in the same tone. (*quickly prepares his reply*) . . . Well, Otun, do you agree?

OTUN (*considering the reply, and translating it*): Though we may be surrounded by numerous people on all sides, being relations, we are sure to recognize and know each other. As we have known each other to be one, we should face each other as relations, and embrace. I shall be seeing you. (*looks at Osi for confirmation*) . . . Well, do you agree?

OSI (*nodding approval*): I cannot agree more.
Osi in turn passes the message back to Bashorun who hangs it on the iron staff tied to the Odan tree.

C

OTUN : Now, comrades, see what a good change fate has brought into these affairs. (*Otun, Bashorun, Kori, Osi and Lape then sing.*)

Quintet

There is someone counting our days
while we sleep.
When we make out our plans
He is also watching;
He can fulfil or foil as he likes.
Life itself is such a riddle
We cannot solve nor denounce!
No matter what today it does afford
Tomorrow it may bring another fate.
Tomorrow we shall build a house
The next a farm we shall make
And up and up we pile our hopes
But God above, He knows the best;
He builds and makes to suit His wish.
Life itself is such a riddle
We cannot solve or denounce!
But joy and grief are quite at par;
So, let us dance and drink and slumber
Lest in sorrow we should sleep.

SCENE THREE

The set is the same as for Scene I with an additional throne and two chairs, placed left and right of the thrones, for Osi and Otun. There are no stools. A golden dagger is displayed at a convenient position on the platform. The time is the same as in Scene One. When the curtain rises, we see a group of eight hunters, worshippers of Ogun (the god of iron), sitting on the stairs of the platform on which the thrones stand. Bashorun and his wife, Kori, are also discovered entering from left down-stage entrance. The leader of the hunters, discovering them, begins the Ijala (Hunters' lyrics) in praise of Ogun and of Bashorun.

LEADER Ogundeji Bashorun son of Ogunsola (*beckoning to his comrades, begins to sing*):

The Ijala (Hunters' Lyrics)

Leader of the Forest lands;
Overseer of the Plain lands,
Great son of our lord Ogun.
Ogun, of earth and heav'n, you are the hunter.
We are hunters in the way of our master,
May Ogun protect our homes.

HUNTERS: May Ogun protect our homes;
May Ogun protect our homes
He gave us guns; he gave us powder,
May Ogun protect our homes.

LEADER: Ogun once came from the hills,
I saw him dressed all in red!
His gown was red – fire-red;
His cap was red, as blood, red.
Powerful god, he can swell and he can burst,
Spit in air; receive it with his eyes,
Annoyed! with both head and tail! he fights!
Ogun please don't be annoyed with us.

HUNTERS: Ogun don't be annoyed with us;
Ogun don't be annoyed with us.
Bad child is never thrown to the lion,
Ogun don't be annoyed with us.

LEADER: We drink freely from the stream,
We sow freely on the farm
For Ogun, the god who gave us the gun
Rules both the stream and the farm,
May he also protect our homes.

HUNTERS: May Ogun protect our homes;
         May Ogun protect our homes.
         He gave us gun; he gave us powder;
         May he protect all our homes.

LEADER: Ogun 'tis you I'll worship,
        There's none other I'll worship.
        Strong god of iron, Ososi's husband.
        Who else but you should I worship?
        Ogun 'tis you alone I'll worship.

HUNTERS: Ogun 'tis you I'll worship;
         Ogun 'tis you I'll worship.
         Strong god, Ososi's husband,
         Ogun 'tis you alone I'll worship.

BASHORUN: Ogun had given me a daughter;
          A husband too he's found for her.
          And there's no husband like the king –
          Son of Gah, respected king,
          May Ogun bless them with children.

HUNTERS: May Ogun bless them with children;
         May Ogun bless them with children —
         The wife's back will not stick to the mat,
         May Ogun bless them with children.

LEADER: Ogun had given him a daughter;
        A husband too he's found for her,
        And there's no husband like the king —
        Son of Gah, respected king,
        May Ogun bless them with children.

HUNTERS (*as the hunters begin this last chorus, Kori and
         Bashorun go into the palace through the arch-way*):
         May Ogun bless them with children;
         May Ogun bless them with children.
         The wife's back must not stick to the mat;
         Ogun, please bless them with children.
         (*all exit through the left down-stage entrance*)

KING (*entering through the large door behind the thrones, followed by Otun, Osi and two attendants*): These things that you tell us . . . (*sits on the throne*) . . . can they be true? That we need make no more scruple demanding her hand in marriage?

OSI: Every word of it, Kabiyesi —

OTUN: And as you have seen, your highness, he has come to consult his daughter about it, and to lay before you his immense apologies for his former opposition.

KING: He should not care to do that. We can see his good intentions; and, if ever we took any offence, it was only on account of our name and position . . . We will see him and his daughter afterwards. Meanwhile, we want her taken out of the inner chamber and dressed up in such a manner as befits the day and our great order. (*to Osi*) Will you see to that, and bring them in when you are ready. (*Osi bows and goes off.*) . . . We must make quite a ceremony of it, don't you think so, our loyal Otun Ajagajigi?

OTUN: Kabiyesi, and arrangements are well at hand to bring all your subjects to witness your highness' wedding.

KING: We will be pleased.

OTUN: I have also — (*enter Kori and Bashorun*)

KING: Ah, ha, here come the parents of our wife. (*to Bashorun, standing up to meet him*) Welcome, my loyal Bashorun, and to you, Kori, mother of our most high prized Derin.

BASHORUN: Kabiyesi, I do not suppose for any moment that I deserve any honour from your highness. But as you so honour us, we proudly acknowledge it. I did not intend to battle with the voice of authority. But now I, and my wife, are prepared to

59

surrender our daughter to your highness – all of her,
alive or dead.
Kori then sings:

Solo

Today my woman's pride soars highest;
Your highness, I shall never forget it.
There are virgins and virgins in your kingdom;
There are maidens and damsels too.
But dutiful Derin excels them;
She is most promising of them all.
As for beauty, she is unsurpassed,
As for cooking, like me she is unequalled –
– My husband thinks I cook better! –
There's no better match for our daughter.

BASHORUN (*with Kori repeating her last four lines*):
As for beauty, she is unsurpassed,
As for cooking, they are both unequalled
– But I rather think she cooks better! –
There is no better match for our daughter.

BASHORUN: Today I feel like a real father –
Whoever took a wife, and in return
Could betroth a daughter to another man
Really deserves the status of a real father.
Dutiful Derin was well brought up
By my hand she's drunk from strictest cup.
As for beauty, she is unsurpassed,
As for food like my wife she's unequalled
– But I rather think she cooks better –
There's no better match for our daughter.
(*Kori and Bashorun sing together, each repeating the last
four lines of respective solos.*)

KING: Humanity is endowed with a lot of gifts.
The one we consider foremost is that of self-
realization . . . My father used to say –

The very first rung in the ladder of folly is to think
oneself wise.' We do not consider ourselves all wise
in the steps we have taken concerning your daughter,
Derin – our most prized wife. But we believe that
we have acted in the way fate would have us do.
If you consider us the best match for your daughter;
we hereby express our gratitude . . . (*then sings*)

Song

Creatures of flesh and blood we are all;
Always staring on a world observable!
We may look, to each other, pre-eminent
Appearing to be confident, and solidly so,
Pontifical – seeming quite infallible,
And apparently being well-to-do.
Within, and in the corners, which others cannot see,
In the corners of our being,
There our hearts, our status – how judged by others! –
Stand faulty! For by faultless self-awareness,
We are lonely, always brooding on our nothingness!
Without this crown worn on our head,
Without our shoes both made of beads;
Without this golden sword here held
– Sign of authority, which also bade us
Occupy the long throne of our fathers –
We would have been a regular brand!
But we won't have drawn just an empty lot
In the stake for Derin's dainty hand.
*At this stage a chorus of subjects appears on the stage
and Derin is solemnly led to the stage by Osi. She is
placed between her parents, while Osi climbs to occupy
his place left of the thrones.*

KING : There are virgins and virgins in our kingdom,
There are maidens and damsels too,
But dutiful Derin excels them;
She is most promising of them all.

As for beauty, she is unsurpassed
As for cooking she is unequalled,
She will bear princes and princesses
Hence our endless love she repossesses.

CHORUS: There are virgins and virgins in your kingdom,
There are maidens and damsels too,
But dutiful Derin excels them;
She is most promising of them all.
As for beauty, she is unsurpassed,
As for cooking she is unequalled,
She will bear princes and princesses
Hence your endless love she encompasses.

OTUN: You have been summoned to this stately Palace
to witness the wedding of our king and Derin.
A palace housing no queen is no Palace,
So, let the drums beat; the wedding bells shall ring.
Meanwhile happy folks —
In the midst of our worthwhile jollity
We'll sing and dance with all hilarity.
And shall each bring the bride a gift;
Her maiden's soul to joy shall lift.

CHORUS: In the midst of our worthwhile jollity
We'll sing and dance with all hilarity,
And shall each bring the bride a gift;
Her maiden's soul to joy shall lift.

OSI: A big 'etu' for the bridegroom,
Damask is for the bride.
A golden crown for the bride-groom,
A head-gear for the bride.
But meanwhile happy folks —
In the midst of our worthwhile jollity
We'll sing and dance with all hilarity,
And shall each bring the bride a gift;
Her maiden's soul to joy shall lift.

CHORUS: In the midst of our worthwhile jollity
We'll sing and dance with all hilarity,
And shall each bring the bride a gift;
Her maiden's soul to joy shall lift.

BASHORUN: This is the most memorable day in my life
– a day when under no compulsion I wed my
own daughter to the person of the king.
Yesterday you all witnessed my disagreement
with the sword of authority; but it is true what the
elders say . . . 'What will be, will be'. Things have
happened to justify that wise saying. Here, in the
presence of you all, I offer my daughter to the king
in marriage. May they live long and happily as
husband and wife. May my lord Ogun bless the
union. May they be blessed with children both
male and female. (*takes Derin by the hand, giving
her to Otun – but before Otun can start moving towards
the throne, Derin kneels and starts the following solo which
is customarily accompanied by sobbing from the bride, and
occasional sighing from the onlookers, especially the
females*)

Solo

DERIN: Thank you for all your cares over me,
Thank you for bringing me up,
May m'lord Orisa also care for you,
May God crown your efforts on me with success.
I am now entering into married life,
Into a home different from my father's home!
How do I behave in my new home?
I know not how they live there —
How do I behave in my new home?
With my domestic duties they may not be pleased
How do I behave in my new home?
If I fail to act in the way they like, I shall be abused.
How do I behave in my new home?

They may not be satisfied with my sweeping —
How do I behave in my new home?
They may not be pleased with my cooking;
How do I behave in my new home?
The egungun of my father's house cannot come
    with me!
How do I behave in my new home?
The orisa of my mother's house cannot come with
    me!
How do I behave in my new home?
Ah, my mother cannot come with me!
How do I behave in my new home?
And my father too, he cannot come with me!
How do I behave in my new home?
Father, mother I am very grateful to you,
For all your cares over me,
For bringing me up so well.
May m'lord's orisa also care for you
May God crown your efforts on me with success!

KORI (*placing her right hand on her head, sings the following
    solo*):

My dear Aduke, I have escorted you enough,
I shall have to go back.
Mothers never follow their children
To their husbands' homes.
I shall have to go back.
When you get into your husband's home
Behave in the way we taught you.
Do not argue with the elder wives of the house,
Behave in the way we have taught you.
Harsh questions and harsh answers
Are the causes of most troubles;
Behave in the way we taught you.
My dear Aduke, I cannot go further with you,
But may my head escort you;
May m'lord's orisa escort you.

Oya will go with you.
Ososi will go with you.
Ogun, great god of iron, will escort you.
Goodbye, Aduke, good-bye.

BASHORUN: Well, Derin, my dear, custom does not
permit me to escort you to your husband's house, so
here, Aderinsola Aduke, we must bid you good-bye.
*As they both solemnly turn to go, Derin begins her
passionate farewell song.*

DERIN (*meeting her parents on the stairs*): Baba mi.

BASHORUN: Yes, my daughter

DERIN: Iya mi . . .

KORI: Yes, my daughter.

DERIN: I shall never let you down. Baba mi . . .

BASHORUN: Yes, my daughter . . .

DERIN: Iya mi . . .

KORI: Yes, my dear . . .

DERIN: I shall be as dutiful
As you always want me to be.

BASHORUN
& KORI: We are very proud of you.

DERIN: I'll be all you wish me to be.
Baba mi

BASHORUN: Yes, my daughter

DERIN: Take care of my mother, father
Take care of my father, mother
Take care of my Aweni,
Of my . . . (*sobs*)
Baba mi.

BASHORUN: Yes, my darling (*patting her on the back*)
Never sigh with pains, my dear,
King will always care for you.
May you never know pains,
May your cares be ever lightened,
Mat will not stick to your back;
You will bear children male and female.
We now wish you all the best;
So, be nice.

BASHORUN & KORI (*repeating last eight lines of duet ending*):
So, good night
And good-bye.
*The King himself who has been standing in rapture behind
Derin, leads her back to her throne as her parents exit
via right down-stage entrance.*

KING: . . . It is interesting the way life treats us all. . . .
What makes others sad makes us glad! . . . So let it
be. The parting of a daughter and her parents
where a wedding is involved means the meeting of
a wife and her husband! Hm, . . . so it is with us
today. (*going to Derin*) . . . She is the only one with a
mixed heart's feeling.
*He bends to wipe her leg with his handkerchief, but she
frowns and resists. Again he tries to hold her by the hand,
but again she frowns and resists. Finally he holds her by
the waist, and this time she smiles and presses closer to
the King who begins to sing.*

King's *Song*

When I touch her leg she's annoyed,
When I touch her hand she's annoyed.
But the beads upon her waist,
Those she offers me to hold,
Those she gladly lets me hold –
This indeed is love all un-alloyed!

FINALE

CHORUS (*females*): Be bright, our Derin, and be cheerful,
The future holds the best for you;
To surpass temptations be at the alert
Other men will long for your hand.
(*males*): Be bright, your highness, and be joyful,
The best of time is yet to start.
To surpass temptations be all alert
Other maidens are around.

OTUN: The code of wedding, it is twofold:
Responsibilities and rights.
To claim your rights and to hold them,
It is right to be responsible.

OSI: The load in the ship cannot capsize it,
But the water around it may do.
So, be strict, and always avoid intrusion;
You must never find faults in each other.

CHORUS (*all*): The code of wedding, it is twofold:
Responsibilities and rights.
To claim your rights and to hold them,
It is right to be responsible.
The load in the ship cannot capsize it,
But the water around it may do.
So, be strict, and always avoid intrusion;
You must never find fault with each other.

KING: It is a happy assignment to rule good-natured
citizens. The honour you have this day bestowed on
us is unsurpassed in the entire annals of kingship in
our land. We shall vividly remember it all the days
of our lives. (*King and Derin then sing a duet.*)

Duet

We shall not forget your warning.
No matter how long we live,
We shall be always longing

To see you every time . . .
To you we owe our joy today,
And hope to pay it back;
While to God our leadership we owe;
We hope to follow His lead.
So good-bye,
We shall see you all again.
So, good-night
And goodbye, bye.

*The wedding procession begins with the couple descending
from their thrones followed by two attendants fanning
them, next come Otun and Osi and, a little later, the
subjects. The procession lasts almost a whole cycle of the
Pavilion: from the throne, in front of the chorus to the right
of it, then down stage towards the audience and finally
exiting through the archway to the other parts of the
Palace. It is accompanied by the Wedding March below
sung by the Chorus.*

Wedding March

ALL : Diyawo, diyawo,
Our pretty Derin marries the King.
O diyawo.

FEMALES : She is fine; she is slim
'Yawo Oba opelenge ni
She is slim.

MALES : He is young; he is king
He wears a golden crown on his head,
He is king.

ALL : How she beams; how he smiles,
Eh eh eh eh eh eh e damuso
How they smile.

CURTAIN

NOTES

Dramatis Personae

KING : He is a descendant of the house of Gahmororo – a
renowned family whose fame as efficient and powerful rulers dates back to the sixteenth century. Even
in the nineteenth century, this King still proves a
true blood. He ardently believes in the divine rights
and authority of kings, and will go any length to
execute his orders. But in spite of all these, he is
very much liked and honoured by his subjects. He
is a young man.

OTUN : Fully titled Otun Ajagajigi. He is next in rank to
the King – his right-hand man. Like his ancestors,
he is a popular poet, philosopher and historian. He
knows the history of almost every family in the land.
Little wonder he has become the leading and the
wisest councillor with years fifty and five to his
credit.

OSI : Fully titled Osi Ajagajigi. He, too, is next in rank to
the King in Council. He is the left-hand man of the
King. He is a shrewd, forty-five year old.

BASHORUN : He is a fervent Ogun (god of iron) worshipper
and believes very much in the guidance of this god.
However, he is unlike the god, understood to be
riotous and boisterous. Most Ogun worshippers,
even today, are boisterous. He too is a chief, and as
Otun sees him, he is 'wise and upright'. He is fifty.

KORI : The name is also that of a god – Kori (god of
children or youth). No doubt the woman of our
play understands children very much. But like
most women, she is vain.

DERIN : The heroine of our play. Young, slim and gentle;
few kings can resist the beauty of such maidens,

especially when they lead the Palace songs. She is a loyal daughter, and very modest in her aspirations.

LAPE : Sister to Bashorun who conspires with her to steal Derin out of the Palace. She is lively, and very daring.

AWENI : Sister to Derin and probably the last-born child of Bashorun and Kori (Derin is their first-born child). Eleven years old. Very fond of Derin.

OGUNMODEDE : As the name suggests, he is an Ogun worshipper, and a hunter. (Ogun brings a hunter with him.) He is the leader of the group of seven hunters. As he himself claims, he knows the god inside out.

Mask entrance

The mask is an imitation of the Otomporo as is played at Ago-Owu, Abeokuta, Western Nigeria. It is an Egungun with some peculiarities. Only part of his body is covered with his flowing robe! The legs, the arms and the face are not covered. He has a long dock-beak. He is closely followed by a man supposed to be his own brother whose face he must not see during the dance, and who also carries the extras of his flowing robe on his shoulder. The legs and arms of both are spotted with white and red paints. The upper arms of each of the followers are also spotted with a single pair of white and red paints. The housewife followers are marked by a long slanting line (nana), red and white, respectively, on each cheek. This is because, being married, they become 'slaves' in Olufakun's compound. In Yoruba compounds, housewives are regarded in custom as slaves of the home children, including even their own children. They are, in turn, children in their own respective compounds.

The instruments needed by this group are the bell (agogo) and the 'batakoto' drum. The rhythm of their music is dictated by the agogo in a—..—.. beat in a moderately fast tempo.

Ritual

The mask play of Otomporo is said to have originated from Ilesha in Western Nigeria. During the celebrations, all male children of the compound of Olufakun assemble for the stick dance. This is usually done when, for example, an elder of the compound dies. For seven consecutive days, the 'slaves' continue to fry native bread (akara) with alligator pepper (atare). The pepper is mixed with the beans for the akara which is fried by using a small calabash to measure the prepared beans into frying oil. Bare fingers must never be used.

On the seventh day, which is when the 'stick dance' is performed, all males get a stick, each measuring about six inches in length and an inch in diameter. As the singing goes on, the sticks are thrown by one person against another. This continues till far into the night. The practice has a story behind it, the relation of which is beyond the scope of this note.

It is this idea of stick dancing which the Otomporo and the king perform during the one-in-three-year's outings of the mask. After the mask has danced round and round the pavilion, he returns to the platform facing the seated king, who spreads his gown to receive the sticks as they are being thrown to him because they must not drop. The mask then throws the sticks (three of them) one after the other. On receiving the third stick, the King packs the sticks, giving them back to the mask. He then joins the mask in the final dance.

Games

(a) The first game, 'Boko, boko', or 'Meet your husband' is played strictly by girls on moonlit nights. The girls sit with out-stretched legs clasping their palms in between their laps. The aim is to deposit a pebble or any other chosen object in one of the clasped palms for the 'Detector' girl to discover. The idea is to declare as ripe to have a boy-friend or husband that Detector who succeeds in recovering the hidden object! It can even be varied by predicting the type of husband the girl will have, and this ranges from a king to his servant or a night-soil-man, all depending on the whim of the Leader. According to the words of the song, she can meet him at the stream, the farm or even in his house! The girl to be so honoured shall hide, or simply just turn her back to the players, while the song is being sung and the object being deposited. The Leader eventually deposits the object as she feigns to do all along. Then she, too, sits like the others calling on the 'Must-Detector' to come out and try to recover the hidden object. If she fails, the leader then recovers the object, giving it to the 'Detector' whose turn it shall be to act as the leading player. She then can choose anyone else to be the 'Detector'.

(b) For the purpose of our play, the second game is entitled 'The King's Order'. The aim is to get the two knees of a girl folded. The idea is that the fortunate or unfortunate girl (depending on what the 'Order' of the king is) has to abide by whatever the king wants her to do.

In this play, there are five girls for the game and therefore ten knees to play on. The game proceeds with counting or touching every knee in turn from the right of the 'Pointer' girl to her left repeatedly and conjointly with the beat of the song. The song has a 1–2, 1–2-time and has forty-nine full beats in all. In this play the two knees pre-determined to fold first are the 9th and 10th respectively and belong naturally to the same girl, Aweni, who sits last, left of the Pointer – Alake. The touching starts with the very first beat of the song which makes it possible for the 9th knee to fold first on the 49th count. After the 9th knee has thus folded, an imaginary knee No. 11

is substituted and pretended to be touched during counts. The already folded knee, No. 9, is not touched or counted during this repeat.This makes it possible for knee No. 10 to fold next and thus concludes the game.

Messages

The particular 'hieroglyphic' message used in this opera is identical in form to the messages which were used by the tribe of Jebu (Ijebu) in Western Nigeria at least until the late nineteenth century. For further particulars, Payne's *West African Almanac*, published in Lagos, 1887, or *The Nigerian Teacher* of September 1936, (8), may be consulted. I have slightly altered the material and interpretation for the purpose of effect in *God's Deputy*.

Costumes

There have not been many changes in the traditional Yoruba dress since the nineteenth century, which is the period of our play. It is true that men's costume is a little more elaborate nowadays. But for accurate presentation of costumes in *God's Deputy*, people producing this play are advised to consult the following: – *A Look at Western Nigeria*, published by the Information Division, Ministry of Home Affairs, Ibadan, under the section for 'The traditional dress'. Note here, in particular, the traditional dress of a Yoruba Oba and his consort. Also, for the ceremonial dress of the Chiefs, see Shell Company's *Nigeria in Costumes* compiled by John Danford. For general variety in the costume of the hunters and male Chorus, see the June 1962 issue of the *Nigeria Magazine*; No. 73. (*Nigeria Magazine*, Exhibition Centre, Marina, Lagos.)

Resurrection

RICHARD RIVE

Richard Rive *was born in Cape Town in 1931. He taught in schools and lectured in the University there and is at present doing a post-gradvate degree at Oxford. His stories have been published throughout the world and in several languages. His first novel,* Emergency *appeared in 1964 and he has travelled and lectured on African writing in Africa, Europe and America. He has edited an anthology,* Modern African Prose, *and contributed to as well as editing,* Quartet, *both published in African Writers Series. A collection of Rive's own stories has been published as* African Song.

CHARACTERS

Mavis, *dark-skinned young 'Cape Coloured' woman*
Ma
The Priest
The Mourners: A fair girl
               A married couple
               A housewife

*The scene is the interior of an emptied dining-room. A
coffin is placed diagonally at front stage to the audience
right. At the foot of the coffin (which is on trestles) is
a chair. Backstage, in the middle, is a crude table, doing
service as an altar, by means of a starched table cloth
thrown over it, embellished with crosses, and a lectern and
open Bible placed centrally on it. Backstage, far left, is
another chair.*

*The time is very late afternoon. The light is grey and
evening is approaching. A time of shadows and meditation.
As the curtain rises a dark girl, Mavis, is sitting on the
chair at the foot of the coffin, oblivious of anyone or anything
around her. On the chair back left an old woman, Ma, is
sitting with her back half-turned to the audience, looking
out of an imaginary window. The sound of singing is heard,
voices singing 'Jesu Lover of my Soul', tremulously at first,
then growing in volume.*

MAVIS: Stop it! Stop it! For God's sake stop!
No, go on. And maybe I'll sing with you.
*The singing is now soft, and the girl attempts to accompany
for a bar or two, then breaks down. The singing fades.*

MAVIS: Maybe sing for you, for myself, and shed the tears
of long ago, century-old time-dripping tears, speaking of my hatred. Come in, all of you, and hear of
my hatred.
*A fair girl comes in, notices Mavis, then goes to the coffin.
She looks in tenderly, then fussily goes out again.*

MAVIS: Come in soft-footed in your starch-white faces,
funeral faces, your pale back-to-church hands;
come with pious prayer-dipped fingers,
and put your flower into the coffin.
Shed one tear, sing a single verse,
perform your solitary duty. . . . for Ma,
Who gave birth to white children. . . . and me.

Jimmy, Rosy, Sonny. . . . and me . . .
*The singing gains momentum, then fades. A couple enters
with a wreath, which one of them places tenderly on the
coffin. Then they too go off.*

MAVIS: Run to your fat homes, and tell your swollen
children,
Your swollen husbands, your rancid wives.
Tell them of Ma, tell them of the Old-Woman,
The mother who was Maria Loubser,
For whom you shed a tear, and muttered prayer.
Maria Wilhemina Loubser,
Black breasts suckling tight white mouths,
And tell them she gave birth to me,
Life to Mavis, who was black like Ma.
Black as Ma's ignorance, like the soil of *Wolfgat*.
The mountain waters of *Wolfgat*,
That flow past *Teslaarsdal* and *Solitaire*.
Black like Ma's ignorance,
The mother before her and the mother before her,
And the mothers before her. (*addresses the coffin*)
You died when you were born, Ma,
We all died when we were born.
You were old in your youth, and grey in your
childhood,
Twisted at birth, warped in your infancy.
You died in the womb, Ma,
Died before you were conceived. (*to imaginary
mourners*) Yes, come in all of you,
Come and say your prayer, drop your flower,
Weep one tear, and weep for yourselves.
Pray for Ma, a prayer for yourselves.
Drop a flower on your own corpses,
Into your own coffins,
Onto your own bodies,
Dead as Ma, black and dead as Ma.
The old woman far left back continues to look out of the

window, then starts to speak, almost inaudibly at first, but her voice gathers momentum as the singing fades.

OLD WOMAN: Mavis!
Mavis looks around without much emotion, then ignores the call.

OLD WOMAN: Mavis!
Mavis sighs deeply, makes as if to go to the old woman, as a reflex action, then resumes her seat.

OLD WOMAN: Mavis, I am calling you, my girl.

MAVIS: Can't you be at peace, Ma, even in your coffin?

MA: Please, Mavis.

MAVIS: I am listening, Ma, I am listening.

MA: Mavis, why do they treat me so?

MAVIS: Why should that bother you?
You are safe enough now.
Why should they bother you?
No-one will touch you now.

MA: Mavis, why do they treat me so?
She gets up painfully, attempting to get to Mavis, who sees her coming and deliberately moves away.

MAVIS: Ask your brats, you made them.

MA (*simpering*): Please, Mavis, tell me my child.

MAVIS (*suddenly attacking her*): Because you're coloured.
You're coloured, Ma,
But you gave birth to white children.
It's all your fault, Ma, all your fault.
You gave birth to white children,
White children, Ma, white children.

MA (*uncomprehendingly*): I don't understand, Mavis, I
       don't understand.
       Why do I smell death, Mavis?
       I smell flowers, and they smell like death.
       I always liked flowers,
       There were flowers in the valleys where we lived –
       Genadendal,
       The valley of mercy, there were always flowers
       there,
       Blue and pink and white,
       But they never smelled like the grave, Mavis,
       They never smelled like death.

MAVIS: You're dead, Ma, dead.
       Don't you know you're dead?
       You're dead and lying in that coffin,
       And they are coming to look at your corpse.
       Coming to look at themselves,
       Because they are dead like you.
       Come over and look at yourself, Ma.

MA (*shrinking back*): No, Mavis, I'm afraid of what I'll
       see.

MAVIS: Afraid to see yourself?
       Come and look into the coffin your children gave
       you.
       Cheap pine, kitchen-table pine,
       Squeezed into your own dining-room at last.
       Your own dining-room, Ma, which was never your
       own.
       Come over, Ma, come and read what is written on
       your coffin.
       *Ma refuses to come but listens wide-eyed. Mavis reads
       the plaque with studied bitterness.*

MAVIS: Maria Loubser: That's your name, Ma.
       Maria Wilhemina Loubser, 1889–1971, R.I.P.

MA (*visibly moved*): Rest in Peace. That's for me, Mavis,
　　Rest in Peace.

MAVIS (*resignedly*): Rest in Peace,
　　With people crowding around, and more people
　　crowding around.
　　Look at the way they are crowding, Ma,
　　Sharing seats and standing in the doorways,
　　Coming to look at you, Ma.
　　Coming to look at the corpse of a broken coloured
　　woman.
　　Can you smell the flowers, Ma?
　　Can you smell the death in the flowers?

MA: It's a good thought, Mavis, rest in peace.

MAVIS: Can you smell the death in the flowers?

MA: I can smell the grave, Mavis,
　　The grave in the flowers,
　　And I can hear the people singing, Mavis.
　　I can hear the death in the singing.
　　*The voices start again, singing 'Jesu Lover of my Soul',
　　then fade.*

MA: They're singing for me, Mavis;
　　Mavis, they're singing for me.

MAVIS (*indifferently*): They're singing for everyone. They're
　　singing for themselves.

MA: Jimmy and Sonny and Rosy . . .

MAVIS: Singing for you. (*turning on her*) Yes, today they're
　　singing for you.
　　Yesterday they cursed us.

MA: Yesterday they did not treat me right.
　　Mavis, why do they treat me so?

81

MAVIS: Do you want to know why?
Shall I tell you why?
Because you are old and black,
And your white children want you out of the way.
They want me out of the way, too, Ma,
Because you made me black.
You made me black like you.
I am your child, Ma, I belong to you,
So they want me also to stay in the kitchen
And use the back door.
We must not be seen, Ma, their friends must not
see us;
We embarrass them, Ma, so they hate us.
They hate us because we are their shadows.

MA: It cannot be true, Mavis, it mustn't be true.
I want to stay in the kitchen.
I do not want to go into the dining-room,
Even if it is my dining-room.
I do not want to meet their friends, Mavis.

MAVIS: You're no longer useful, Ma,
You're a bloody nuisance, a bloody, nuisance.
You might come out of your kitchen
And shock the scum they bring here,
You're a bloody, black nuisance, Ma.

MA: But I don't want to sit in the dining-room,
It's true, Mavis, I don't want to sit in the dining-
room.
*Ma cries silently and helplessly. Mavis makes no attempt
to help her, as the old woman tries to get to her
daughter.*

MA: It's my dining-room, Mavis, my dining-room.

MAVIS (*turning brutally on her*): You're black and your
bloody children's white.

Jimmy, Rosy and Sonny are white, white, white!
And you made me,
You made me black!

*Mavis forces Ma into her (Mavis's) chair. She herself
walks to the window out of which Ma had originally
been gazing, struggling to contain her emotions. Then she
breaks down and runs to the old woman, weeping in her
lap. Ma does not understand the breakdown, but soothes
her daughter, speaking to her, and as the old woman gets
into her theme, her voice, from being shaky, becomes
stronger and more perceptive.*

MA: At the side of *Grootkop* is a sandy path,
A narrow path which is filled with bush.
And higher up are the mountains of Caledon,
Caledon and the Little *Karroo*,
Cool and grey-cool in the evening,
And on the other side of the path
is a deep kloof, a deep gorge,
And at the bottom flows sweet water —
shallow water in a deep gorge —
Laughing over brown and white stones.
And the water runs all the way to Solitaire,
And *Karwyderskraal*, where the ivy climbs over
the beautiful Moravian Church
And makes it more beautiful.
And the moon rises rich and yellow
From the hills behind *Grootkop*
And in the evening,
In the heavy-breathing Karroo evening,
With door tight shut, we would sing the songs of
long ago. *(She starts singing)* Slaap my kindjie slaap sag,
Onder die engele vannag . . .
Come, Mavis, come my child,
Take me by the hand and let us look at the moon.

MAVIS *(resisting)*: One must not look at the moon.
I belong in the sun. I must look at my sun.

It is not good to look at the moon.
*Voices again start singing 'Jesu Lover of My Soul'. A
housewife enters and goes to the altar. She lights the two
candles; then, crossing herself, goes to the coffin and looks
in. The fair girl comes in, consoles her, and they go off,
ignoring Mavis and Ma, who are frozen in their accustomed
positions.*

MA : The sun has set for all of us, Mavis,
    There is no sun.
    It is a time for shadows.
    Grey and deep they lengthen across the room,
    Shading our half-lives, greying our souls.
    And listen, Mavis, listen carefully,
    Through the shadows you can hear singing,
    The misty tunes of yesterday;
    Shadow music, the grey notes of long ago,
    Can you hear the singing, Mavis?

MAVIS *(her indifferent self)*: I can hear the singing.
    I can hear you. I can hear them singing.
    *The voices gather momentum for a bar or two, then fade
    away.*

MA : Please, Mavis.

MAVIS : I told you I am listening.

MA : Why do they tell my friends not to visit me?

MAVIS : Do you want *Soufie* with her black skin to sit in
    the dining-room?
    Or *Ou-Kaar* with his kinky hair?
    Or *Eva* or *Leuntjie*?
    Do you want your son's wife to see them,
    Or the dirt Rosy picks up?
    Do you want to shame your children,
    Humiliate them? Parade their blood?

MA : I only want my friends to visit me,
    They can sit in the kitchen.

MAVIS: And what of my friends? What of my coloured
friends?
Must they also sit in the kitchen?

MA: Mavis, I do want my friends to visit me,
Even if they sit in the kitchen.
Please, Mavis, they're all I got,
Ou-Kaar and *Eva* and *Leuntjie*,
They're all I got.
We were children together, Mavis,
Where the narrow path is filled with bushes,
And the cool gorge runs deep below,
Where the shallow waters laugh over white and
brown stones,
We were children together, Mavis.
We would pick the reeds and lump red oxen out of
clay,
Thick and red, from the red mud of the river.
And at *kinderfees*, Mavis,
At the feast of the children, and at Easter,
We would dress up in our best,
Our Sunday-going-to-church best
And go to the Moravian chapel,
Where the lamps hang from the tall roof,
and mellow the church,
And makes the singing more beautiful.
Ou-Kaar and *Eva* and *Leuntjie*,
we would make the singing more beautiful.
And are they also here, Mavis?
Are they here and singing for me?

MAVIS: They're sitting in the kitchen where they can't be
seen.

MA: It's not right, Mavis, it's a sin.
They should be singing for me in the dining-room.

MAVIS: In the kitchen where they can't be seen,
Frightened and timid, where they belong.

Soufie in a new *kopdoek*, sizes too big,
And *Ou-Kaar* in yellow boots borrowed from somewhere,
Come, Ma, come and see *Leuntjie* with her twisted
leg.
Come and hear *Eva* speaking the raw guttural Afrikaans
of the Caledon District.

MA: They are my friends, Mavis,
Your mother's friends.
They are the friends of my childhood,
The friends of the valley of mercy.
We grew up together, my child.
It is not right to mock them.

MAVIS: Bring them into the dining-room, into your
dining-room,
And shock Dadda's friends and relations.
Leuntjie and her twisted leg,
And *Eva* and her guttural Afrikaans.
Do you want them to sing with the people
Who ignored you while you lived,
But know you now in death?
Death brought you into your dining-room.
They saw you and did not see,
Heard you and did not hear,
Felt and did not feel.
Watch them, look at them,
Pawing over your coffin, strangers in life,
And friends in death.
Relieved by death.
See them peering into the coffin
Of their friend's black wife.

*Ma refuses to look into the coffin and shrinks back. Mavis
resumes her seat at the foot of Ma's coffin. The housewife
reappears with two vases of flowers. These she proceeds
to put on the altar. The fair girl comes in and rearranges*

wreaths and flowers on the coffin. The place is obviously
crowded as both of them recognize people. The couple also
come in, pass a few words and go out again. The fair
girl and the housewife also exit. During all this the
singing continues.

MAVIS: You see, Ma, how they work for the dead,
　　　　And ignore the living.
　　　　Dead for the dead,
　　　　For the barriers belong to life.
　　　　Barriers which part mother from daughter,
　　　　and sister from brother,
　　　　and love from love.
　　　　But death integrates,
　　　　The dead with the dead,
　　　　The living who die with the dead who died,
　　　　So now you are at last in your own dining-room.

MA: But they knew, Mavis, they knew,
　　　They knew I was dying.

MAVIS: They knew you were dying from the day you were
　　　　born.
　　　　And I knew they knew,
　　　　I saw it in their eyes.
　　　　But I was afraid, Ma, I was afraid.
　　　　Afraid of you, afraid of your children,
　　　　Afraid they would turn and say,
　　　　'Clear out of our house,
　　　　You bloody bastards, you bloody black bastards,
　　　　Clear out, both of you!'
　　　　But I was most afraid of myself.
　　　　Because I knew I would then have cleared out.
　　　　Should then have cleared out.
　　　　Looked for a room in Woodstock or Salt River,
　　　　Walked the slopes of Signal Hill, beyond the Malay
　　　　Quarter,
　　　　And forgotten my humility and frustration,

The compressed hatred bundled inside,
The bubbling volcano.

MA : But I did what was right for all my children,
For you and all my children.

MAVIS : You did more than that,
You sent them to a white school.
You were proud of your brats,
And you hated me, Ma, hated me,
For you saw yourself in me.
You encouraged them to bring their white friends to
the house.
To your house, to sit in your dining-room,
While we remained in the kitchen,
And you had a black skin yourself.
We were becoming one, Ma,
One in suffering and ignorance, growing together.
Now we are one, you are me, and I, you.
So they pushed us both into the kitchen,
Because they saw one, not two.
There's no-one to blame but you,
You're to blame for all this, Ma.

MA : I do not understand, Mavis, I cannot understand.
Why do they treat me so?
Mavis, why do they treat me so?
Why must I live in shadows,
When I gave them the light?
Why do I live in shadows?
Deepening, grey, then darker.
Tears, flowers and handkerchiefs,
Are they for me, Mavis, are they really for me?
The tears, the flowers and the shadows?
Are they singing for me, Mavis?
White people singing for me?
*The voices continue singing 'Jesu Lover of my Soul'. Ma
listens carefully while Mavis remains indifferent.*

MA: I know it's for me because I am dying.
Maybe I'm already dead,
Mavis, I want you to see to my funeral.

MAVIS: Ask your brats to bury you.

MA: They are my children, Mavis, but they do not treat
me right.

MAVIS: Do you know why? Shall I tell you why?
Because they're ashamed of you, afraid of you,
Afraid to tell the world of their mother.

MA: But I did my best for them.

MAVIS: You did more than your best, you encouraged
them,
But you were ashamed of me, weren't you?
So we shared a room at the back.
Come and look at the world which was your kitchen
Where we can't be seen.
And you are going to die,
And maybe you are already dead,
And your white children will thank God
That soon we will both be out of the way.

MA: They are your brothers and sisters, Mavis.

MAVIS: What's that you're saying? What's that?
I hate them and I hate you!
I hate you!

MA: But you are my children, you are all my children.
Please, Mavis, don't let me die so.

MAVIS: You will die in the back-room and be buried
from the kitchen.

MA: It's a sin, Mavis, it's a sin.
But I am not lying in the kitchen, Mavis,
That's me in the coffin, Mavis,

Here in the dining-room,
My children have put me in the dining-room.

MAVIS (*ironically*): Your children have placed you in the
dining-room.

MA: And they are singing for me.
Listen and you can hear my children singing for
me.
Voices continue singing, then fade.

MA: And see, Mavis, they are all coming in,
Even *Ou-Kaar* and *Leuntjie* and *Eva,*
And Sonny and Rosie,
And Dadda's friends and relations,
Dadda's white friends and relations.

MAVIS: Yes, Dadda's white friends and relations.

MA: Mavis!

MAVIS (*indifferently*): Yes?

MA: Please, Mavis, see that Father Josephs buries me.

MAVIS: Ask your brats to ask him.
See them ask a black man to bury you!

MA: Please, Mavis, see that Father Josephs at the Mission
buries me.

MAVIS: It is not my business, you fool,
He did nothing for me,
You did nothing for me.

MA: I am your mother, my girl, I raised you.

MAVIS: Yes, you raised me,
And you taught me my place.
You took me to the Mission with you,
Because we were too black to go to Dadda's
Church.

Let your children see our priest for a change.
Let them enter our Mission and see our God.

MA: Please, Mavis, let Father Josephs bury me.
*A white priest enters in cassock and surplice. The room is
obviously crowded as the priest recognizes and greets many
present. He takes up a position behind the altar. As he
moves the singing rises to a crescendo, then fades as he
raises his hands in prayer.*

MA (*very impressed*): It is the priest from Dadda's Church,
But I wanted Father Josephs to bury me.

MAVIS: You have a priest from Dadda's Church,
A white priest from Dadda's Church.
Let him pray to his God
For the salvation of a black soul.

PRIEST: Let us pray.
*Mavis resumes her seat at the foot of the coffin. Ma in her
seat, sobbing silently, overcome at the religious implications.
The priest addresses not only the imaginary mourners but the
auditorium as well.*

PRIEST: 'I said I will take heed to my ways
That I offend not in my tongue.
I will keep my mouth as it were with
a bridle: while the ungodly is in my sight.'
*Mavis looks up, fascinatedly, staring at the people around,
then at the priest. Ma's eyes follow Mavis in a bewildered
fashion.*

PRIEST: 'I held my tongue and spake nothing.
I kept silent, yes! even from good words,
But it was pain and grief to me.
*Ma can hardly control herself. Mavis watches the priest
entranced.*
'My heart was hot within me, and while I
Was thus musing, the fire kindled, and at

91

the last I spake with my tongue.
I heard a voice from heaven, Saying unto me,
"Write:
From henceforth blessed are the dead which die in
the Lord;
Even so saith the Spirit, for they rest from their
labours" . . .'
Ma rushes over to Mavis and cries silently at her feet.
The people are singing softly in the background.

PRIEST : Lord, take Thy servant, Maria Wilhemina
Loubser,
Into Thine eternal care.
Grant her Thy eternal peace and understanding,
Thou art our refuge and our rock.
Look kindly upon her children,
Who even in this time of trial and suffering
Look up to Thee for solace.
Send Thy eternal blessing upon them,
For they have heeded Thy commandment,
Mavis slowly rises to her feet; Ma, a crumpled heap at
the foot of the coffin.

PRIEST : Which is,
'Honour thy Father and thy mother,
That thy days may be long . . .'
Mavis is on her feet. The singing stops abruptly while
Mavis stares aghast at the priest who seems oblivious of
her presence. He remains with his hands outstretched, in
suspended prayer. There is an ominous silence, then Mavis
speaks hysterically.

MAVIS : Misbelievers! Liars!
You killed me. You murdered me!
Hypocrites!
Don't you know your God!

CURTAIN

Life Everlasting

PAT AMADU MADDY

Pat Amadu Maddy *is a Sierra Leonean, born in 1936. During the 1960s he worked in Britain and Denmark, where he produced plays by African writers for Danish radio. He has also been a producer with Radio Sierra Leone. In 1969 he was responsible for training the Zambian National Dance Troupe for Expo'70. He is working as an actor in London and has been in theatre, television and radio productions. A collection of his plays has appeared under the title* Obasai *(AWS 89).*

CHARACTERS

Big Boy, *Servant in Hell*
Mr K. Abibu, *ex C.I.D. Superintendent*
Mrs Selina Mcarthy, *Housewife*
Pastor Simeon Collins, *ex-Clergy*
Voices, *singing offstage 'Are We Punished for Our Sins?' 'Are We Punished by Our Sins?'*

Life Everlasting

*The action of the play takes place in a very small, un-
decorated room. No furniture. It's bare, and creates an
effect of indefinable nostalgia. Left alone in this room,
one has a feeling of claustrophobia. In effect this room
symbolizes the illusion of Hell. The play opens with Abibu,
a Negro about 33 years old, crouching on the floor, howling
like a frightened dog. Selina, a young Negress, tall and
beautiful, is also half-lying on the floor, purring like a cat.
Pastor Collins, kneeling as if in prayer, grunts like a pig.
These characters are dead, and are put together as Destined.*

BIG-BOY : Good afternoon, Good evening, Good morning,
Good-day . . . This is Hell . . . we are in Hell,
where we never say good-bye . . . those who come
here . . . when they are here . . . here in hell . . .
they are here to stay.
*Abibu, Selina, and Pastor Collins unconscious as they are,
begin to produce animal sounds as described in their
characters.*

BIG-BOY : There is not that much marked difference here
in Hell as it is on Earth . . . (*animal sounds rise and
interrupt*) . . . Quiet, my friends . . . (*shouts*) . . .
Quiet, I say, you God-forsaken demons. (*silence*) . . .
(*Big-Boy laughs a very strange and unusual laughter.
This can be very irritating and embarrassing.*) . . . That's
better. Silence is, as they say, golden – sometimes . .
Now we can stop being animals. . . . put aside your
animal instincts and let's get down to business. . . .
Let's get to know each other better. . . and our
purpose of being put together here . . . here in Hell.
When once you are here, which doesn't happen by
chance . . . Nothing happens by chance . . . NEVER
. . . There is nothing like the so-called, personal-
contact main-man. No favouritism, no priorities,
nothing whatsoever of the kind . . . You are here,
and you are here to stay for all time through eternity.
(*pause*) . . . Strange things happen here in Hell . . .

the great, the weak, the mighty, the learned, the
poor, the sickly, the bastard, the legitimate, all
mingle together regardless of their sex, their class
and their race. . . .

SELINA: Gosh . . . it's hot in here.

ABIBU: It's no use complaining, open the windows darling,
and draw the curtains.

BIG-BOY: I'm afraid there are no windows here, no
curtains to be drawn.

ABIBU: And who the devil are you, may I ask?

BIG-BOY: My name is Big-Boy.

ABIBU: Big-Boy be damned . . . what the hell are you
doing in my bedroom?

BIG-BOY: I see you are still not quite awake . . . still not
aware of where you are.

PASTOR: Where is my Bible, Sally? . . . Why did you
move it? . . . I have always told you not to touch
my Bible . . .

SELINA: I am not Sally. My name is Selina.

ABIBU (*confused*): Hey . . . you, what did you say your
name was again?

BIG-BOY: Big-Boy . . . my name is (*spells it slowly and
calculatingly*) B.I.G.B.O.Y.

ABIBU: Big-Boy?

SELINA: Big-Boy.

ABIBU: Wha . . . what kind of a weird place is this?

SELINA: It's not only a weird place . . . it is a strange and
weird set-up.

ABIBU : I asked you a question. (*shouting, commandingly*)
What kind of a black-hole is this?

BIG-BOY : This Sir, is Hell.

ALL (*except Big-Boy*) : HELL?

BIG-BOY : Yes . . . Hell.

ABIBU : To hell with you.

BIG-BOY (*laughs*) : That's where you are, Sir . . . This is it
. . . Hell.

ABIBU : Who are these people?

BIG-BOY : They are your Comrades . . . we are all
comrades in arms . . .

ABIBU : Is she my wife?

BIG-BOY : No.

ABIBU : Who is he? With the Dog-collar?

PASTOR : I beg your pardon?

ABIBU
SELINA } (*together*) : Who are you?

PASTOR : I should be asking you the same question . . .
What are you doing here?
Big-Boy laughs heartily.

SELINA : Stop.

ABIBU : Shut-up.

PASTOR : Quiet.

BIG-BOY (*stops*) : As you wish . . . I see you don't have
any sense of fun.
Footsteps can be heard approaching along the corridor.

SELINA : Someone is coming.

BIG-BOY: He is not coming here.

SELINA: Who is he? . . What is he doing? . . Where is he going?

BIG-BOY (*repeats her questions*): Who is he? . . . He is nothing . . . What is he doing? . . . Nothing . . . Where is he going? . . . Nowhere . . . He is Nothing . . . but Nothingness . . .

SELINA: Quiet . . . Shhhhhhhhhhhhhh.
Steps become heavier and distinct with great calculated thudding.

SELINA (*quietly*): I am scared . . .

ABIBU: Shut . . . (*footsteps thud heavily and stop.*)

PASTOR: Let us kneel in prayer. (*prays alone*) Forgive us our trespasses O Lord, and lead us not into temptation, but deliver us from evil . . . and from human wrath and bondage . . . give us peace in our time O Lord. Amen.

BIG-BOY: I would have liked to join you in your little prayer, pastor, but we don't pray here in Hell . . . we have got no time for such trifles.

PASTOR: Trifles? . . . You call prayer trifles?

ABIBU: Look Mr Big-Boy, or whatever your name is, I don't like this kind of kids' game . . . I don't play games . . . open that door: I want to get out, out of here.

BIG-BOY: Games? Who is playing games? Who is behaving like kids?

ABIBU: Look, maybe you don't know who I am . . . I am Chief-Superintendent of the Sierra-Leone C.I.D., and the name is Karimu-Abibu . . . so just you don't try to be smart.

SELINA (*shouts*): Help . . . get me out of here . . . police (*hysterical*) Police . . . we have been kidnapped . . . lynched . . . help . . .

BIG-BOY: It's no use shouting, madam . . . here no-one can hear you. This room is sound-proof, besides, here in Hell no-one interferes with whatever is going on in another block.
Different animal sounds can be heard from outside. Pigs, lions, bears, snakes, dogs, birds, monkeys. All come in simultaneously and clear. Last of all the frogs.

ABIBU: What are those funny sounds?

BIG-BOY: Ah! Those are your neighbours.

ABIBU (*frogs still croaking*): What? (*surprised and shocked*) Frogs!

BIG-BOY: Yes. Frogs, snakes, lions, birds . . . etc . . . etc . . . etc. They are your neighbours . . . we don't practise segregation here.

PASTOR: Here? . . . Where?

BIG-BOY: Am sorry Pastor, I keep forgetting, that you are still not quite used to the idea that you are in Hell.

PASTOR: Me? In Hell?

BIG-BOY: What's wrong with that?

PASTOR: Many things . . . why should I, of all people, be put in Hell? and what is the meaning of having animals as neighbours?

BIG-BOY: There is no difference between you and the animals, Pastor. They have their souls to save as you have. In fact they've got quite used to it . . . and they are very happy. Very adaptable those animals are . . . funny how it is, that it is only puny little mankind who never gets used to his unexpected circumstances, and to any immediate change of his stereotyped situations.

SELINA (*pleading and crying*): Please . . . do, Big-Boy, do get me out of here, please . . . set me free . . . set me free . . .

BIG-BOY: It is not within my power to do such a thing . . . I am here like the rest of you, like you three . . . and we are here, and here to stay.

SELINA: We will never get out of here?

BIG-BOY: Never.

SELINA: Why? Why? Why?

BIG-BOY: Because you are all Dead . . . all of you. This is where you have to have your eternal rest.

SELINA: What about you? Are you dead too?

BIG-BOY: No. I am different from the three of you.

SELINA: How?

BIG-BOY: I was never what you call flesh and blood . . . I have always been here, always will be . . . here.

SELINA: How do you explain that?

BIG-BOY: Well, it's simple . . . for the three of you to meet here, in this particular room, specially designed for you, here in Hell, there must be some One here to make sure of your arrival, and that you arrive safely, when you have completed your earthly assignments. So, I was put here, in this little room, from where I can watch you . . .

SELINA: And you have always been here?

BIG-BOY: Yes, always . . . watching and waiting for the three of you.

SELINA : What did you do, what do you do while you watch and wait?

BIG-BOY : Oh, I sleep sometimes . . . but still in my sleep I was aware of your movements . . . the three of you.

SELINA : Why has it got to be the three of us?

BIG-BOY : Destiny. You were destined to live together in life-everlasting . . . life after death.

SELINA : But . . . but . . . we don't know each other?

BIG-BOY : Ah well, that is part of my job.

SELINA : What is part of your job?

BIG-BOY : To make sure that you get to know each other, and this is as good a time as any other, to start observing our little, but very important, formalities.

SELINA : Formalitics?

BIG-BOY : Ycs, we observe and practise our own formalities here in Hell . . . as you are used to, down there in the green pastures. Now, I take it you all know my name by now?

SELINA : Big-Boy. Isn't it?

BIG-BOY : That's right.

SELINA : Were you born and baptized here, Big-Boy?

BIG-BOY : Oh, no . . . We don't get baptized here in Hell . . . We have no time for such unnecessary trifles like baptism and marriage – no time for such trifles. However, you have all the time you need to find out all you want to know about everything that happens here in Hell.

SELINA: Will you always be here?

BIG-BOY: Yes, I will always be here . . . always (*pause*)
Now for the first of our little formalities . . . Introduction.

SELINA: What did you say?

BIG-BOY: The first of our formalities, the formalities that
we should observe.

SELINA: What is that?

BIG-BOY: Getting to know each other by name – who
and what we are – and the purpose of our being
assembled here.

SELINA: You call this an assembly? We are caged, imprisoned . . . in this . . . this *den* . . . surrounded by
reptiles and wild animals and birds.

BIG-BOY: Time will help you get used to the idea . . .
Now, your name is Mrs Selina Mcarthy.

SELINA: How did you know that was my name?

BIG-BOY: It is my job to know . . . later I will explain
myself, and in what capacity I am here. This is
pastor Simeon Collins.

PASTOR: You have told me that I am dead, that I am in
Hell, that my prayers are trifles, that frogs are my
neighbours. Now you are telling me my name . . .
What will you be telling me next about myself that
I don't know?

BIG-BOY: I will be doing very little telling and talking,
Pastor. It will be left entirely up to the three of you
to do all the talking and telling, and the general
Findings-Out.

SELINA: What will you be doing?

BIG-BOY : I never know what I am going to be doing next; nor do any of you as far as I know. Now for our comrade over there.

ABIBU : Don't call me 'comrade'! I am not a bloody communist. My name is Karim Abibu, and I have told you that before.

BIG-BOY : I don't know about the pastor and the lady. Maybe they wouldn't like you to use such a strong word as 'bloody'. But for me, I don't mind if you swear, you can use all the swear words you know . . . What we don't appreciate, here in Hell, are the accepted goodly virtues. There is no difference, here in Hell, between the good and the bad, the ugly and the beautiful, the perfect and the imperfect, the weak and the strong, the sinner and the saint . . . Oh, no . . . Here they are, all the same kind, the same rank and file. Their names are all in the One big Black Book.

ABIBU : You don't have to tell us. Everything seems to be very well worked out and organized . . . It is all quite clear.
Same footsteps approach again.

PASTOR Is anyone else coming?

BIG-BOY : No, Pastor.

PASTOR : Is it going to be just the three of us? and you?

BIG-BOY : Yes, Pastor.

PASTOR : But you said, earlier on, that there is no discrimination practised here in Hell.

BIG-BOY : I said segregation.

ABIBU : Damn it, man . . . segregation . . . discrimination. It's all one and the same: two words with the same meaning.

BIG-BOY: Maybe you are right, Mr Abibu. But I wouldn't know. I did not go to school like you.

PASTOR: Where do white people go when they die?

BIG-BOY: Where they are destined to go, Pastor, it is all in the big Black Book.

PASTOR: I see.

SELINA: Give me a glass of water, please, I am thirsty.

BIG-BOY: Water? Thirsty? Sorry, Mrs Selina, we don't have water here in Hell.
Footsteps thud clearly, then stop.

SELINA: That Nothing . . . Nothingness . . . he is out there again. (*whisper*) Water, give me water. (*hoarsely*) Water, I feel choked.

ABIBU (*whispers*): Quiet . . . I . . . I . . . feel scared . . . I'm sweating . . . it's never happened to me before, like this . . .
A moment's complete silence.

ABIBU: I . . . mean, I have never been afraid of anything. Never.

BIG-BOY: There's no need to be afraid or frightened. . . . You are all quite safe in here . . . well protected . . . secure. No harm, no danger will ever come to any of you.

PASTOR: How do you know that?

BIG-BOY: It is my job, my responsibility, Pastor, to protect all of you . . . Also I have been put here as a servant, to do as you all wish, to wait upon you all, hand and foot . . . to advise and inform you as to *how* and *why*, you are here.

ABIBU: Why are we here?

BIG-BOY: Well, to begin from the beginning . . . We must first learn how to live in peace and harmony. To achieve this, or to be able to succeed in conceiving this, we must unite as ONE. To be able to unite as one, we must get to know each other, communicate with each other, understand each other, and last of all, and most important, LOVE each other.

ABIBU: And how do you suggest we set about achieving this grand proposition?

BIG-BOY: TIME, Mr Abibu. Time is the greatest and most important factor, and you have endless time here in Hell to be able to find out how to set about achieving this Grand Proposition.

ABIBU: Endless time . . .

BIG-BOY: Yes, endless time . . . that is what you have a lot of here, here in Hell. We are not going anywhere . . . We are not in a hurry . . . no rush . . . We never run short of time here.

ABIBU (*sarcastically*): I'm sure we never will . . .

BIG-BOY: As you can see, comrades, we don't worry about anything here . . . nothing. Whether physical, mental, moral, or intellectual. You had all those things to worry about down there in green pastures. You strived to live and rise up to the great expectations demanded of you, within the short life-span you had to live. Your green pastures was a world of disturbance and confusion . . . time was against you. In your mad rush and unconditional confusion, you forgot what it was like to live, and love each other.

PASTOR: I have always loved my flock.

BIG-BOY: It is not for you to say, Pastor.

PASTOR: But I know.

BIG-BOY: We will soon find out, Pastor.

ABIBU: Are you telling the pastor that he is lying?

BIG-BOY: The pastor had better ask me that question himself . . . However, as I was saying, we must learn, rather begin to learn, how to love each other. That is the Purpose of you all being put together here.

PASTOR: The four of us?

BIG-BOY: No Pastor, the three of you. I am just a servant.

PASTOR: Just a servant?

BIG-BOY: Yes, just a servant . . . your servant . . . so make sure you use me, and use me well! (*pause*) *The hooting of an owl is heard, long and forceful.*

PASTOR: What's that?

ABIBU: Tell that bloody owl to shut up.

BIG-BOY: I can't. He is doing his job. He is informing us, that we are having another . . .

ABIBU: Another what?

BIG-BOY: Another comrade. *Hooting continues in the background.*

SELINA (*hoarsely*): Is this other comrade coming here?

BIG-BOY: Yes . . . he is coming to Hell . . . but not to this room.

SELINA: Shh-hhhhhhhhhhhh. (*in a whisper*) Can you hear voices?

BIG-BOY: It's on behalf of our new comrade that is coming. His relatives and friends are paying him their last tributes.

SELINA (*quietly*): Quiet, look, look at them.
> *From a distance can be heard a bell tolling as in a*
> *cemetery during a burial. The sound of the bell rises and*
> *becomes clearer; the bell is rung five times with definite*
> *pauses between. Singing Voices rise from the background*
> *as the last bell is rung.*

VOICES (*singing*): My brother where you're going to?
> Am going to the Lord.
> My brother where you're going to?
> My Lord calls me.
> We will meet by the river Jordan.
> Singing glory, glory, glory.
> We will meet by the river Jordan
> You are bound for Canaan land.

PASTOR (*the pastor is the same as pastor Collins. A symbolic image*):
> The Lord gave and the Lord has taken away,
> blessed be the name of the Lord.

VOICES: Amen.

PASTOR (*chanting*): Let us pray . . . Enter not into
> judgement with thy servant O Lord, for in thy sight
> shall no man living be justified. If we say that we
> have no sins, we deceive ourselves and the truth is
> not in us, but if we confess our sins, he is faithful and
> just to forgive us.

VOICES: Amen.

PASTOR: Grant, we beseech thee, O Lord, eternal rest to
> our dearly departed brother. Let perpetual light
> shine upon him, O Lord, and bring his soul to
> rest safely in thy heavenly Kingdom.

VOICES: A.m.men.

PASTOR: May his soul rest in peace.

VOICES: Amen.

PASTOR: May the angels of God lead thee into paradise
. . . in your journey, may the martyrs receive you
and bring you safe into life everlasting . . . may the
heavenly choir sing you unto eternal rest.
*Sound of a coffin crashing down six-foot hole. Sound of
mourners crying.*

BIG-BOY: Very exciting spectacle. I watched these funeral
ceremonies every day, especially when I waited for
you.

ABIBU: You didn't have anything better to do?

BIG-BOY: Anything better to do? What a thing to say. I
keep telling you that here there is no super-standard;
nothing better than the other, no-one is better than
the other . . . animals, birds, you, me, the lady, the
pastor, this room . . . it's all the same, all the
same . . . (*bursts into laughter*) for ever and ever. All
will always be the same . . . timeless and lifeless . . .
all will always be the same.
*Cacophony of animal and bird noises, then a pause. Big-Boy
freezes. All goes quiet. He stands speechless and reacts to
nothing that the other characters say.*

SELINA (*panicky*): Why does everyone keep quiet? (*pause,
then shouts*) Say something one of you. Say something. (*pause*) I can't stand this quiet. (*tensely*) This
room makes me sick. I will go mad if I stay here any
longer . . . It's Hell . . . it's sickening. (*shouts*) Say
something, don't just stand there gaping. Pastor,
you can at least pray. Pray just to break the
monotony of this nauseating silence . . . pray (*pause*)
you . . . you Mr Abibu . . . you are a policeman,
a C.I.D. man, arrest me, get me out of here . . .
take me to your cell. (*shouts*) Go on, arrest me!

ABIBU: But you have committed no crime.

SELINA (*tensely and panicky*): Oh yes, yes I have. I will confess, if you will promise to arrest me. Go on, promise that you will . . .

ABIBU: But I can't.

SELINA: Yes, you can . . . you will, you must. You are the law . . . you must execute justice. I must be punished.

PASTOR: You are now being rightly punished, daughter, for your crimes. It is no more to do with man-made laws, it is in the hands of yourself – you are your own judge; your own juror; your own prosecuting and defence council – and we are here to do the same.

SELINA: And that Big-Boy over there, is he to witness all that we have to confess?

PASTOR: No need to worry about him, he knows everything about us . . . more than we know about ourselves.

SELINA (*crying*): I'm scared. What shall I do?

PASTOR: Confess and make peace with your soul, my child . . . Your soul's concerned, my child, your soul's concerned.

SELINA: Will you help me? Will you try to understand?

PASTOR: That's why we are here . . . to learn to help each other . . . to try and understand, and to be able to love each other.

SELINA: It was all her fault, she asked for it, and I gave it to her.

PASTOR: Whoever it is, don't blame it on her, blame yourself. It is common among the living to blame their fellow men; it should not be so with us.

SELINA: What did you say, Pastor?

PASTOR: Your friend, I say you have no right to blame her.

SELINA: You mean Daisy? Oh, Pastor, you don't know her, she was not my friend, she was my greatest enemy. She took my husband away from me, yes she did, she made him hate me. She turned his head, and heart, against me . . . She gave him love medicine . . . She ruined my home.

PASTOR: What did you do to her?

SELINA: I couldn't bear the scandal, the shame, the gossips. Oh the humiliation! He took her everywhere . . . they made so much fuss over each other, even in my very presence, and on very many occasions. The whole thing was no secret. He was going to divorce me and marry her . . . she scorned me in the streets, laughed at me in the market, and put her friends up to jeer at me, to mock me, everywhere I went.

PASTOR: Did your husband love you?

SELINA: My husband treated me with contempt, because of that Daisy – she was young and attractive.

PASTOR: Did you make your husband love you? Did you show him that you loved him?

SELINA: He wouldn't talk to me . . . he hardly came to the house . . . whenever he did, it was only to change his clothes. To him I was just nothing. Nothing. I pleaded with him to come home. He refused . . . he wouldn't hear of it.

PASTOR: So?

SELINA: So . . . (*crying*) so Daisy was expecting his baby
. . . his baby . . . Not that I couldn't have a baby.
(*crying*) Knowing that if she had that baby, that
would be the end of our marriage . . . so I, I
decided once and for all to have it out with her . . .
I thought of many different ways, then in the end
I decided to do it the painless, but expensive way –
I paid Pa Kemoh, the Herbalist, and he did it.

ABIBU (*commandingly*): What did he do?

PASTOR: Easy, Mr Abibu, easy.

SELINA: He put out her candle, as the saying goes.

PASTOR: Killed her? How?

SELINA: Yes, I killed her . . . she died sweating.

PASTOR: How did you kill her?

SELINA: Well; Pa Kemoh conjured her image to appear
on a very small mirror, which he gave me to hold
in my left hand; he then gave me a small
thunder-hammer in my right hand. When the image
of Daisy appeared on the mirror, all I had to do
was bang! with the hammer, the mirror breaks into
pieces. That very instant Daisy was a dead corpse . . .
yes . . . dead. (*crying*)

PASTOR: But, but Selina, my child . . .

SELINA: Don't sympathize with me, Pastor . . . I don't
need sympathy . . . I did it. I alone did it. I can
see it all now . . . I did it because I hated her . . . I
hated Daisy. She came between my husband and
me . . . she . . . spoilt my happiness . . . my love . . .
(*crying*) all that belonged to me, she deprived me of
. . . she stripped me naked . . . left me with
nothing . . . absolutely *nothing*. Do you understand?
DO YOU UNDERSTAND!

PASTOR: Yes . . . yes, I suppose I do.

SELINA: Now, Mr Abibu, you will arrest me . . . you will
. . . you must.

ABIBU: But how can I? I am here just like you, with an
impure soul . . . I'm here, and here to stay, as
Big-Boy said. I am nothing now, not even a
super-numerary policeman, just a lifeless, timeless,
ungodly spirit, doomed, condemned into perpetual
isolation and torture . . . (*shouts*) Can't you see, we
are being tortured? look at him! Do you think he is
not looking and laughing at us? Call him . . . go on,
call him!

PASTOR (*calls*): Big-Boy . . . Big-Boy . . .

SELINA (*calls together with the pastor*): Big-Boy . . . Big-
Boy . . .

ABIBU: Why do you think he just went quiet all of a
sudden? Go on, answer! Talk, talk, Big-Boy . . .
you know why we are here – to be tortured. Why?
Why should whoever it is want to torture our souls?
. . . our bodies lie deep down in the grave. Six
feet, deep down below the stinking, scorching brown
earth; as mere food for worms. Yes, that's what our
bodies are now, just food for earthworms. Isn't
that enough? Why shut three souls together in this
blasted dungeon? (*shouts*) Set us free . . . free . . .
free . . . let my sin-stained spirit wander wherever it
may choose to go.

PASTOR: You were a man of the laws, Mr Abibu, you
know, as well as I do, that breaking the laws,
man-made laws, for that matter, is punishable by
fines, imprisonment and even death penalties.

ABIBU: Yes, I know that.

PASTOR: Well . . . man-made laws can only punish the body. Here in Hell, where we find ourselves without knowing how or why, the Master Creator, the All Powerful Force, punishes not the body, but the Soul, the Spirit.

ABIBU: I feel naked and empty . . .

SELINA: We are all naked; naked spirits.

PASTOR: No. We are not naked . . . we are clothed with the garments of our sins – our unpardonable sins.

ABIBU (*fighting with his emotions*): Sins . . . sins . . . sins! Christ Almighty, I did sin. (*gnashing his teeth*) I sinned all right. Well damn it all . . . I did it. It was my duty as a police officer, as a senior member of the police force, to protect the interests of society . . . Christ, you cannot have well-established law and order in any country, without enforcing it. People think the worst of a policeman just because he is a policeman. Why?

PASTOR: You are not a policeman any more.

ABIBU: I know. People *must* respect the Law. They asked for it . . . they *made* it. They must respect it; they must respect the policeman. By Christ, if I could be born again and had to live my life through again within the police force I would still do it all over again, if I had to . . . Justice, the Law, Order, Respect . . . Order and Decency, all must be observed within a good society.

PASTOR: Society? Do you still think of it?

ABIBU: I can see it all . . . all of it. Society, I shocked society, I sent my own mother to prison . . . I arrested her for disobeying the law . . . yes, I did.

SELINA: What did she do?

113

ABIBU: I warned her . . . I did warn her many times . . .
she wouldn't listen. In the end I took her in, just
like anybody else. (*pensive*) Strange woman she
was! 'Dear Mamma', I said, 'You are coming down
with me to the police station for brewing home-made
illicit gin.' I wasn't joking, and she knew that I
meant it. She just smiled . . . a smile she kept until
the day the judge sentenced her to three months
hard labour. As she did *not* resist arrest, so she did
not put up any defence, no force, no resistance,
nothing. She *smiled*, just a plain, cold crooked smile
. . . Yes – my own dear Mamma – I stood and
watched her go to jail, as I have always watched
others go.

SELINA: You did that to prove what? I mean, what
prompted you to do such a thing? Why did you do
it?

ABIBU: I had a job to do; my job.

PASTOR: Get down on your knees and pray, Abibu. Pray
and ask God to forgive you.

ABIBU: Pray? I don't know how to pray, Pastor. I have
never prayed in all my life; when I had flesh and
blood, when I was a man, the real living Karimu
Abibu, I never did go anywhere near a mosque or a
church . . . I was just another ruthless, worthless,
hard-hearted disciplinarian, teaching other people
how to live; when in fact I was the one who needed
to be taught how to live.
Big-Boy laughs, a prolonged laugh.

SELINA (*shouts*): Stop.

BIG-BOY: It is part of the formalities that I should
laugh – when I want to – it will help you to purge
your iniquities.

SELINA: Quiet . . . listen.
Footsteps approach as before.

BIG-BOY: I will always interrupt your confessions from time to time.

PASTOR: Why?
Footsteps become clearer.

BIG-BOY: There is no reason why.

ABIBU (*shouts*): Quiet!
Footsteps stop outside.

SELINA (*pause*): Is he coming here?

BIG-BOY: I keep telling you not to worry – no-one is coming here. No-one will ever come . . . NEVER.
Footsteps thud a few steps, then stop. Pause.

PASTOR: Listen to that . . . it's stopped. (*shouts*) Who is it? Come in if you want to . . .
Footsteps thud away slowly.

PASTOR: Tell him, whoever it is, that keeps sending you – (*shouts*) can you hear me? Tell him that we are here, and here to stay; to be tortured, to be spied upon, in whatever way that is necessary for us to be treated.
Animal noises from outside.

ABIBU: Damn those animals, damn the whole lot of them.

SELINA: They are our neighbours . . . our neighbours for all time.

PASTOR: For all time . . . ai, so it is, for all time. Doomed to live next door to the Spirits of animals and birds. (*they all laugh, Big-Boy tops their laughter*) For heaven's sake be quiet all of you . . . (*shouts*) Quiet . . . (*pause*) How dreadful . . . dreadful to live in such a black-hole . . .

BIG-BOY: Even if you had not sucked on the milk of prosperity and had been weaned away from the hocus-pocus of flesh and blood: you'd still have had to live in this black-hole, Pastor.

PASTOR: I was a man of God. A holy man. A leader of the Flock. I preached the Word as written in the Holy Gospel. I preached it to all and sundry – to all races, creeds and every nationality. I baptized the young, as well as the old, anointed the sick, and the dying. United the separated, encouraged the downhearted, had pity on the poor, gave advice to the rich – I did as the Book says.

ABIBU: Your faith let you down, Pastor.

PASTOR: I let my faith down. Now here I am . . . in hell . . . a wretched no-good-for-anything clergyman, a cast-away sinner. No more salvation for me, none whatsoever. I did not kill or imprison anyone physically, but I did commit a worse crime.

SELINA: What?

PASTOR: My soul harboured resentment for my own Bishop – he was a much younger man compared to me – less experienced, more successful. He had all the great qualities of an upright, and diligent, man. For me, he was a stumbling block, a thing in my way . . . I received him with open hands and beaming smiles . . . while, in my heart of hearts, I detested him. My joys, my peace, my future were all a matter of great importance to me . . . I wanted to be a Bishop myself.

SELINA: What happened in the end?

PASTOR: I wished vainly, and my wish was not fulfilled; I left nothing untried in my unfruitful restlessness of wanting to become a bishop. I ascended the dizzy heights of anticipation . . . hoping, and praying fervently. The days came and went by, the mornings and the evenings came, but the day I wished for, and desired most, never came.

ABIBU : But still, you went on, praying early and late, preaching and teaching?

PASTOR : I made every effort . . . In the end, my long-nourished hope and wish began to decline; time went on as it always does; I gave up to the stupefying exhaustion of my bitter sorrows. I wallowed in my false pride, and hateful resentment. My busy thoughts became weary . . . the illusion that once delighted my eyes, and exalted my heart's desires, became a sombre, macabre spectre; now it's no more . . . no more. It waned to less than emptiness . . . empty nothing . . . no more . . .

ABIBU : No more . . .

SELINA : No more . . . What will happen to us here?

PASTOR : Nothing, nothing at all, except what is happening now. . .

ABIBU : . . . and no-one will ever come to rescue us?

PASTOR : No-one. Never.

SELINA : And we will never get out of here?

PASTOR : Never. This is our Life-Everlasting . . . Our Salvation.

ABIBU : How strange: how funny. If only one of us could go back to earth and tell the others what it is like here, on this side . . .

PASTOR : Yes . . . to tell them that there is no river Jordan . . . no Canaan Land . . . except . . . except . . .

SELINA : Have faith, my friends. . . .

> *Selina bursts out laughing. The others do likewise. Their laughter becomes hysterical and uncontrolled. A gradual fade. Animal noises come in to top their laughter. There is a pause. Thudding footsteps approach. All goes silent, footsteps become clearer, then all stops.*

CURTAIN

Lament
A radio play

KOFI AWOONOR

CHARACTERS

Spoken in the first production by:

First Voice, *A woman in her twenties* (Valerie Murray)
Second Voice, *A man in his thirties* (Cosmo Pieterse)
Third Voice, *A very old man* (Kofi Awoonor)

The time and place are relatively indeterminate, but the setting is a generalized African one, and the period fairly contemporary. Mime, dance, movement, slides, silhouettes or colour can be used in addition to the three voices.

Lament

FIRST : That night he came home, he came unto me
at the cold hour of the night,
Smelling of corn wine in the dawn dew.
He stretched his hand and covered my forehead;
There was a moonbeam sparking rays in particles.
The drummer boys had got themselves a goat —
The din was high in the wail of the harvest moon.
The flood was up gurgling through the fields,
Birthwaters swimming in floods of new blood.
He whispered my name in a far echo;
Sky wailing into a million sounds
Across my shores. His voice still bore
The sadness of the wanderer —
To wail and die in a soft lonely echo.

SECOND : Your tears are running like the flood river;
They are as bitter as the waters of the sea.
Why are your eyes so red?
Do you cover your head with your hands
And tremble like the orphan child by the roadside?
I shall leave you
So that I go to perform the rites for my gods.
I shall weave new sisal ropes
And kill two white cocks,
Whose blood will cleanse the stools.
The bitterness of your tears
Still lingers on my tongue
And your blood still clings to my cloth.
The winds of the storm have blown,
destroying my hut.
Goats came and did a war dance
On the fallen walls of my father's house.
What happened before the vulture's head is naked?

THIRD : They do not know it;
These infants from the strength of our loins
Do not know it.
If you turn your neck,

121

Look at the whole world:
The heat and the restlessness,
How drunken dogs are
trampling precious things underfoot,
And stray hyenas carry their loot
to the cleared patch in the forest;
Tears will gather in your eyes.
Though they said
The prince should not hasten for the stool,
And the young leopard
Should not be in haste to walk,
But noises are in the air.

FIRST: That echo I had heard long ago
In the fall of night over my river,
In the distant rustle of reeds,
At growth in the strength of my river.
Once upon an evening I heard it
Strung, clear as the gong of the drummer boys,
Bright-burnished like the glint edge of
The paschal knife, ready-anxious to cut
My cords and enter into my fields.
I was still a dream then,
Carried by the flimsy whiffs of
Sweet scents, borne aloft on the vision
of my coming flood
That will bear me slowly and gently
into his world of strength and smells.
He was not very gentle with me.
But I did not complain. The thrust
Was hard and angry, severing the tiny cords,
Shattering the closed gates of raffia,
Gathering at its edge the reeds to feed my fishes.
My flood had not risen,
The canoe carried on the strength
Of his man, rowed steep down my river
Into a tumultuous eternity

Lament

Of green hills and mountains,
That reeled and rolled to the river shore
To clasp and bear me away.

SECOND : The path to the farm is long,
Very, very long.
The earth worm ate our new yams
And left the skins near the smithy shop;
The smithy shop is on fire, my people,
It is on fire.
Remember the day the smithy shop caught fire,
Remember you who are in the smithy shop?

THIRD : My people, where have you been?
And there are tears in your eyes.
Your eyes are red like chewed kola,
And you limp towards the fetish hut.
My people, what has happened:
Before, you bear many cudgel wounds
And rope marks cover your naked bodies?
Wipe away your tears
And knock on the door of the sacred hut,
The gone-befores are waiting for you.

FIRST : Then the flood gates opened
in sluices to cleanse, to purify
My evening of awakening,
in the turbulence of his triumph,
into the bright evening of my rebirth.
The birth was tedious;
The pangs were bitter.
Into the bright evening I rushed
Crying 'I have found him, I have found him'.
He stood there rustling in the wind;
The desire to go was written large upon his fore-
head.
I was not ready for his coming,
I was not ready for his loneliness,

For his sad solitude against the rustling wind.
I was not ready for his entrance
Into my fields and shores of my river;
The entrance of raffia was closed,
Closed against his lonely solitude.

SECOND: The gourd went to the river
And never returned, what will the young ones do?
And when the ram died not
Could the ewes perform the ceremony of weed . . .
That day they opened the sacred hut,
And made pledges to the gone-befores,
I was there.
They wound a cloth around my loins
A fly-whisk in my right,
And a calabash in my left hand.
I was there
When we pledged to the ancestors,
And swore the oath
That you do not thirst for drink
When your palm trees are prospering.
That day we killed the sacred ram,
And the thunder drums sounded,
I was there.
I put down my whiteman's clothes
And rolled a cloth
To carry the ram's head
And go into the thunder house.
When you started the song,
I sang it with you.
My steps fell in
With the movement of your feet to the drums;
I put my hand in the blood pot with you.

THIRD: I heard the voice of a gun,
I came to have a look:
Who are those?
Who are those saying

Lament

They have surplus gun powder
And so we cannot have peace?
I met Agodzo by the roadside,
A net on his shoulders,
Complaining about the sea being bad these days,
So his wives have run away to marry strangers.

FIRST : He stood beneath my entrance;
In his approach I knew the steps he took,
Like the departing Lazarus
Marching towards his grave.
I was not ready.
The flood was gurgling at the estuary
Swimming within me, birthwaters
Warmed by his coming. He was silent,
Mute against the rushing of the wind,
To cry and die for his homeland.

SECOND : If I had known . . .
If only I had known,
I would have stayed at home.
I would not have followed the trancers to another
   land
That cannot give me food to eat.
It was the season of burning feet;
Those who stood around the ring laughed
And said my feet had blundered
And our land had lost the cunning of the drum.
We answered them
That the cow asked the vulture:
You are an uneatable bird,
Why are you so full of your own importance?

THIRD : It has happened again:
The swooping eagle does not give to its child
So the child must turn a beggar in the market
place.

Brave warriors come and hear,
If the gun refuses to fire
Is it not the conservation of gun powder?
There is war in the land of the dead
And ghosts are doing a war dance,
Marching with drums towards the land of the
living.

FIRST: My flood had not risen then.
Across my vastness he marched into the wind,
His hand folded upon his chest,
His eyes searching for the gates
That will open his amulets
to snatch and wear his talisman of hope.
His march into the wind,
Howling through door posts,
To catch the boatman at the dawn point
to ferry him across my river.
But I was not ready.

SECOND: Listen, my countrymen, listen:
The bush fire burnt the bush
But did not touch the bush rope,
Where has it been heard before?
Call my god of songs for me
That he will start a song for me
I have a song to sing
I will sing it before death comes.
Let me be under the trees
And it will thunder,
I will hear the voice of thunder.

THIRD: The heroes, the heroes, where are they?
Where are the war heroes?
Did they smear themselves
With the blood of fowls?
And are bellowing, bellowing
Like wounded hippoes . . ?

Lament

When I spoke in public
They said I was drunk with gin;
My rich neighbour spoke in public
They said his wisdom is great
And the elders shook hands on it.
I put my canoe on the river
I want to go beyond.
The river is wide, very wide —
Then I saw two bamboos
Dancing on the wide wide river —
What shall we do?
Some say we must cover our heads
With our hands, and burst into tears,
But I will not cry;
I shall put on my smelly cloth
And speak in the market place.
If the elders protest
I shall ask them, ask them
That when the sea was sterile
And the poor died of hunger on Modui hillock
Where were you?

SECOND: Tell Agonyo that I am coming;
The singing voice I have
I have it from the gods.
Those who cannot bear my songs
Let them patch their ear holes with clay.
Listen, my people, listen
And I shall sing a song of sorrow —
Some day, by some rivers,
I shall sit down among the elephant grass
And hear the estuary roar
Till the end of time.

FIRST: My hands stretched to cover his
in the darkness, to cover his eyes
in the agony of his solitude . . .
So call his names. I knew

127

to put the dressing from my womb
on his cudgel scars,
to hold his hands in the clasp of night fall.
He was mute, the wind had stopped rustling,
He was erect like the totem pole of his household,
He burned and blazed for an ending . . .
Then I was ready. As he pierced my agony
with his cry, my river burst
into floods, my shores reeled and rolled
To the world's end, to where they say
at the world's end the graves are green.

CURTAIN

Ballad of the Cells
A physiology in 27 pulses and a choral elegy

COSMO PIETERSE

Cosmo Pieterse *was born in 1930 in South-West Africa. After graduating from Cape Town University, he taught in South Africa for eleven years before going to teach in London. Besides writing scripts, poems and reviews, he produced and acted in plays both on stage and for radio. He has also edited* Ten One-Act Plays *(AWS 34), and co-edited and contributed to* Protest and Conflict in African Literature *and* African Writers Talking *(Studies in African Literature, Heinemann), as well as* Voice and Sound: Nine Radio Plays. *He has compiled* Seven South African Poets *(AWS 64) and also* Five African Plays *(AWS 114). He is now Associate Professor in the Department of English, State University of Ohio.*

CHARACTERS

Narrators 1 and 2
Looksmart Ngudle (L.) *an African Prisoner*
Four Interrogators (Int.) *White Special Branch/Political
Police Officers*
Voices of Crowd
Woman's Voice
2 Children's Voices

Ballad of the Cells

Main setting: a police interrogation cell where Looksmart is being cross-questioned. As he recalls various scenes in his life the shifts of background to the Transkei, Cape Town, Worcester, Pretoria, the Drakensberg range of mountains, the Johannesburg gold mines, the Vaal river etc. can be achieved through blackouts and slide projections in a stage production.

PULSE 1

NARRATOR: Alone;
    His ghost haunts me,
    Nor will it leave you alone
    Till his restless corpse
    Tall spirit
    Is grown
    Beyond dark taunts in
    Fenced cities, bitter dorps
    To its own bright station
    Within our possible time
    That we will inherit
    The ageless all we
    Whose reasoned elation
    Is rhymed, timeless, sublime:
    And his spirit a sole
    Elegiac tree
    Whose far roots fuse
    To its tall stem
    Past and present and whole
    And its rhythmical leaves
    On branches of loves
    That labour for use
    And tomorrow lives
    Dividual mass
    Clusters and cells
    Spring budding and birth
    Ripe time, flower's death

And the high hymn
And the hard seed
Simple pure rhyme
Plural coiled sound
Birds sing on
Swallow and swan
Eggs of the phoenix
Finch, pelican
Canary and man
Birds sing on
Their will winging
Sing on the wing and
Over all lands
And over the epic nest
In the poised
Pinnacled noiselessly
Perfective cypress
That may move grains of soil
In our earth, and compass
Even round space
And space so high
In the wind and its wide
World wandering voice
Over green graves
Which hold the rest
Of the nameless brave
Whose unknown death
Seed stifled in sand
Find symbol and name
In Looksmart's last breath
His deathless zest
Living timeless gust:
Individual time
Rings,
And rings
That time won't toll,
But will chime

Names and his mates
His mate
And his name
And sings
His all
Love, faith, his mate
And hope
Though alone . . . . . .
Without sleep,
And alone
He waits
In general where sections are in **bold** *but lacking
quotation marks, the voices of interrogators are to be
understood and to be assumed as containing enough physical
or emotional force to be translated into echoes of varying
strength in the mind of 'Looksmart' Solwande Ngudle, the
'90-day detainee' who is finally found dead in his cell.
The Interrogator's is the voice of two or more policemen
jeering and jibing at the man in the cell ('Looksmart'
Ngudle), and at times professing sympathy and
understanding and offering advice. A tormenting voice
always echoes phrases from the Interrogator's remarks,
statements or questions in Looksmart's subconscious.
For Looksmart – the use of quotation marks indicates
actual speech; where Looksmart 'speeches' lack quotation
marks, he is thinking, soliloquizing.*

PULSE 2

L : No married love beside my sleep
    Only bland mirrors multiply
    Glib answers hollow echoes keep
    Wide silences reply and die.

L : 'I am no criminal. I'm a man.'

INT : **You are a man. Quite. All is well.**

L : 'Why kraal me as an ox alone?'

133

INT: **This is your cell; no kraal, nor hell.**

L: No feet beside my pacing, halted march
    Only dim murmurs that divide
    My mind from me and overarch
    The cell where Looksmart tried and died.

L: 'The world's beside: We're not alone.'

INT: **Alone? No, not alone. Alone.**

L: 'They hear my cell, our country groan.'

INT: **And stand aside; leave you alone.**

L: No man is islanded if hope
    Oceans his lone peninsula.
    Some armied hinterland trains slop-
    Ing hills, 'trains . . .'

INT: **What trains! Where?**

PULSE 3

L: 'Rails gleam the addered distances
    That summer's speed sloughs off in time:
    The winter's sleep: resistance is
    The ultimate this life must rhyme:
    A spring tensed now against your crime.

PULSE 4

L: 'Against two children cradled in my arms,
    And both my arms; for manhood speaks:
    (Both ambushed arms, and all at rest . . .)
    Present arms, fall out, stand at ease? –
    All arms embodied every day;
    Days grow to all the lengths of weeks
    Throughout the weakening of the moon,
    And every month aches yearning time.
    Bulls gore red earth, my daughter's blood.

The round year spills its month of days:
The madnesses of lunar length
That drain the country of its men:
Three months are ninety days that drag
Through Worcester's trained valleys of vine;
The mountains of the witch are high
But valleyed with autumnal time
And valiant for the round sky's dome.'

PULSE 5

L : High flat Karroo:
    Dry roof:
    Dull mouth of fear;
    Wide house of drought
    Dead leaf . . .:
    Autumnal year;
    Dumb, windy flood . . .
    Where am I here?
    Why I
    Why am I I
    Why
    Here
    Without my time
    And sphere
    Across a cross
    Traced by
    The snake's riveting length.
    Tranced by
    The river's snaking eye
    That trails
    The rails
    And wings of flight
    Trans-
    Vaal
    Or
    Kei

The prey-filled flame
The bright
Hawkeye
The fielded mule-yoked ox
Hokaai
My child.
Why
Wife
And where
The summer
Rained:

PULSE 6

L : 'Green frogs gurgling hurrahing storms;
    The purple quiet of this night
    Assumes tubular hollow, hidden forms
    Of lucent moonbeams, soundless flight

    Where moths were celebrating light
    The nuptial dance of earth and warm,
    Pure, sunslaked space, freed from the tight
    Cocooning coil, the larval lust.

    The stormy, pulseless dongas stream
    Continual the veinous clay;
    Blue nightmare lungs of ocean suck, leak, swim,
    Cough blood, sink; seaweed greens away.'

PULSE 7

L : Away
    Another cell
    Of life
    Away
    Ebb briny tide
    Blue moon
    Of blood
    My barren wife

The brackish spring's
A city
Oh! a way
Of life
Away
On swell
Of ocean's waters
Pity
Sway
Of ocean's fall
Spring's nubile
Daughters
Sand
And
Dead day

PULSE 8

L : Groined flesh is warm
    Round circled walls
    The angled wall
    Is cosily and moistly soft

    But cobwebs sit
    And subtly spin
    And stalk
    Light to design and dust to sift
    Branched shadows dancing patterned silk
    The spider's hair, eyed, spun, is talk
    'Four walls
    Of lonelinesses
    Baulk':

PULSE 9

INT : **Your room's this single, yellow eye,**
    Inflamed with sleepless tongues that pry.

L : 'My father's home will keep me sane.'

137

INT: **Your father's home! The mission bells . . .**

L: 'The homing cattle lowing rain . . .
Smell the fresh streams, full wells. . . . ' **What else?**

INT: **Huh? What except an empty-wombed,
Weeping and darkly-longing love?
Fresh streams brim rich. But you are roomed
Here in this cell, without. . . . all love.**

PULSE 10

L: 'My love's a city's floral flame at night;
Paint's colour sung through gusts of time;
The focal breath of beaming light, a name;
My tawny lioness rhymes all her lust,
Still haunting mine.

A flower and an animal,
A parable, a decimal,
The integrating swell, the fall
That matter drains sub-minimal.'

INT. 2: **Absolute bull:
Created by love's abstract fool.**

L: 'My love's the candled aloe hour that blooms
Over stone tortoise shelled for peace;
Green gleaming lights, gloom on the land;
Flames soon released from hell,
Not daunting mine.'

INT.3: **If the afflatus just ain't divine
Call Bacchus and at 10 to 9
You're bally certain sure to sign:
Spirits are willing, and so fine
Distilled in magic-cough brandy-wine.**

L: Florence and Mona
Ray, Leonora
Essence and aura
Earth and its daemon

Ballad of the Cells

Leon and Lionel
And Leonardo
Lone tortured beauty
'Jamilla and Helen'.

INT (*with Looksmart joining in aloud*): **Is love that fabled
town whose tragic face was** 'woman's labour and
man's ' **Work
Eden after the glistening snake
Laocoon's peristaltic pythoned guts
Hercules writhing in his shirt**
'The leaping flames whose lust and' **Grace**
'Make' **Classic Marble** 'of' **our** 'names, the dirt
And rubble of this shame, our' **Pain and** 'smuts'.

INT: **Oh, now you're politicking, boy?
Well, watch your step.**

INT. 1: **We'll tell you how
The gradual mountain-climbing saint of peace
Whose integrating mind forsook
His nation, used his slow degrees
To loose dark death;**

INT. 3: **And also Bondelzwart, Bulhoek.**

L: 'We knew the subtle snake that crawled
Past Kasteel's Poort's altars of stone;
We knew the fanged, forked tongue that called
Death's voluntary apple meat, and bleached the
bone.'

PULSE 11

INT. 4: **But we . . . . today we speak as man to man.
We give you votes, government, land.**

L: 'Yes, Bah! bah! Black man
Will you get a vote?
In 'Yes Baas' – Baahntustan
Of sheep-in-sheep's coat

Chief – Caesar – Headman
Foot – man – fool
Of the brand-new ethnican-
Niballistic school!'

INT. 2: **Damn your bloody cheek, you . . . .**

NARRATOR: Lightning hands
Turn the dumb cheek's unsluicing blood
To blind, gashed anger, but the sands
Of pain absorb the lonely flood.

INT. 2: **'Who are the Jews that paid you, Kaffir?'**

L: They're named – democracy and hunger.

INT. 3: **'Which coolies raped your naked mother?'**

L: Redress her congressed limbs, my love, my anger.

INT. 3: **'What bastard Hotnot's guts can fight?'**

L: Freedom has chartered many freights.

INT. 2: **'Blackbum Kaffir, ham's son of night!'**

L: Time sings, and strikes: (Midnight!) and waits . . . :

L: (A single moth could give me life:
Moths came from shadowed places. Here
Blank walls are raped by blind, cold light.
Warmth has no still, cool places here.)

INT. 4: **You heard that . . . . . Y. Gave evidence!?**

L: Herds of battle, birds of our will.

INT. 4: **You have heard . . . . . Z. by any chance?!**

L. 'Yes, I have heard. Be still!'

PULSE 12

L: Names sing a melody
Timeless amorphous

Ngcika and Kreli
Caved Batwa, Dingani,
Bambatta and Ghandi
Conducive to norms
Surnames and nicknames
Forms, farms, times! fames
Notions, names, nations
(Amandhla!) Isawandhla
Assagai's impi
Shield, axe and kierie
Drums of our feet
And the arms of our mind
Mandela, September,
Bunting and Cissie
Bardien and Barney,
Sisulu, Luthuli
(Uhuru!) Maburu
And names sneer disharmony
Arlow, Barlow, Botha
Sickness on malady
Coop our coffins
Iron pounds gold
Grey, Hertzog, Rhodes,
Silence enormous
Smuts, Tulbagh, Malan
Breaking our forms
Invasions of time
In clamour cacophonous
Strijdom, Matanzima
Gold, silver, copper,
Nossel, Vinoos, Golding:
What forms for names!
And names to rhyme forms:
'Moses Kotane said . . . . .'

INT. 3 : **'Caught any fish today?**

INT. 4 : **'C'mon, Looksmart, you're a clever fellow.**

**Make a statement, man. Don't be yellow.
We'll protect you from . . . .'**

L : The rainbow's arch
 Green, violet, rose;
 Time's forward march?
 And my eyes close . . . . .

INT. 1/3 : **Come, fellow, come
 Don't play the dumb
 Senselessly numb
 Games you opossume.**

INT. 4 : **'Open your eyes . . . .
 Yes open your eyes, Ngudle, look . . . .'**

L : My eyes are inward, still.

INT. 4 : **'This statement must convince you that we
 took . . .'**

L : 'Life from us, land, love, will.'

PULSE 13

(Light from us gone
To give us terror;
Lion and buck from tawny
And tall green forests of fire.

Moths in the mirror;
Curtains are drawn:
Reflection on fur or
The nightmare of dawn?)

INT. 4 : **'Do you hear us?'**

NARR : He stirred,
 His lips were a whimper;
 His will was so limp a
 Whisper concurred:

L : 'I hear you . . . . I hear . . . . I have heard . . .

PULSE 14

L : 'I have heard . . . . song
        People sing'

SOLO-SINGING : All over this land:

CROWD-SINGING : Boss is in the parlour
        Afrika!
        Mayor Police Mission
        Games Game Liquor
        Parliament in session
        Laws or wette

Still – Nkosi sikelele
        Xhosa, Nama, Zulu
        Afrika!

Hear the bells all tolling
Sponono – wam
        Afrika!

Our mares are foaling
        Jonah – yo!
In the park that mists are
        Covering still

So – Nkosi sikelele
        Swazi and Ndebele
        Coolie, Pondo, Sutu
        Griqua, Coloured, Jew, Maburu.
Oh Nkosi – all abantu
For aba-ntu are men

SOLO : It won't be long
        When bells shall ring
        All over this land.

L : 'Yes, I have heard
        That man is man
        For all time
        Each name, all colours and all lands. . . . . . .'

143

SOLO & CROWD: S: **Then** C: Hisa Moya
                              Come now spirits
                              Joyous pleasure
                              O'er erst desert
                              Till our future
                              We'll fear nothing
                              Law's in

                    Our fair land

                              O'er men
                              Oh! men
                              O – Men
                              Ah – men:
                              All men are men.
                              Amen

L :'I am a man.'

PULSE 15

INT: 2: **'The bastard's fainted. Kick his guts'**

NARRATOR: Dull pain suffuses half-dead dust
               Until redoubling life is thrust
               Through each foot, on the groin's moist ruts,

               Upon held hands shocked into fists
               In sharp, electric cataracts, in fits
               That flood the spasmed body, rake
               Poor naked, tortured earth to rock
               Of muscle that succumbs to pain's
               Hailstones of words, showering rains,
               Whipping blind questions through his face:

INT. 2: **'Trust Coolies? Or The Bastard Race?**

INT. 3: **'Babis who fleece you through the year
         In filthy shops, of hard-earned pence!**

**And coons cavorting from their fear
Of life in Tweede Nuwe Jaar's wild, lurid
prance?"**

L : 'New Year was music, and no class
Of man exists or will; we all sang there, together,
danced,
And earlier levelled living grass,

INT. 3 : (**All flesh is grass, your bible says!**)

L : And later while limbs fused and glanced

INT. 2 : (**'A fucking blown fuse. What damn jazz!'**)

L : And lit the laughter of new time
Where foot and hand and mouth will rhyme
Heaven's promise, all-arching rain:
'Past lands, well ploughed, will husband time's new
gain',

The suburb sang and Table Bay
Swerved passionate and graceful waves
Beneath the mountain's austere grey
As day broke pearly in its caves.

New Year devoted us to years
Resolved to new years' rising slopes:

L. & ECHO to INT. 1 : **Fundraising parties. That house
. . . Where . . . 'Where?'**

L : My silence sings, my fancy gropes

INT. 4 : **'A white suburb?' Could you live there!**

L : My life did, friends, our plans, our hopes . . .
(*From this point the voices of Interrogators 1 and 4 fuse
with the thoughts of Locksmart from a gradual interruption
to the point where what they say is the burden and his
thoughts are only an echo of their statements.*)

'What plans?' Dark subway. Sprayguns.
'Who?' Who told . . .
To shoulder **Tell-tale** hills while he
'While he perhaps kept safe *his* home?
May tunnel safely home; while he . . .

'Duplicity deploys disciples dumb
Jews' Judas silver, stock and pile e-
rode your land. Gold shares. Shares?
They rise and ride. You stay their arse.
They rise and ride you! And you come
Dumb bumpkin uncle Tom Jim John Boy come
Come don't be a fool.' While he . . . Why lea
ve them safely stay at cosy home
Home stay your home
Why stay at home
Safely they home
Father sane home
Here have as home
Warm smoke in home
Ho . . . Smo . . . You schmo . . .
'Say No!'
   Old Wily
     Gnome
Au tata – wam
Home Heaven heaven home
   'Smoke?'
   'Ta.'
   Ah

INT. 4 : **'Ah! Yes, your father's home will keep you
sane.'**

L : My father's home? The mission bells?

INT. 4/1 : **'The cattle low, glisten home rain,
Smell the rich milk, full udders, . . .**

L : 'And what else?'

146

PULSE 16

INT. 1/3 : **Summer, and sun, and lazy, drowsy sin,**
　　　　　　and joys
　　　　　　Where bees and buds make dizzy houses
　　　　　　flowers,
　　　　　　The lion's honeyed sweetness stingless flows
　　　　　　Out oozy gourds of gold.

L : 'Yet life empowers
　　　　Slaves to sing empires low;
　　　　Worker bees to sting their drones;
　　　　Joshua's trumpet shrill to blow
　　　　Strong arms and lips to blast high thrones,
　　　　Building the days greener, to grow. . . .

　　　　Cells to besiege invading germs;
　　　　Guerrilla war to choose its single terms;
　　　　Till peaceful flutes and roses glow . . .'

INT. 3 : **Day after day you sweat away**
　　　　　Gorilla wherefore in who's zoo?
　　　　　While that plucky Sam Kahn,
　　　　　Wily Yusuf Dadoo

INT. 2 : **Sit faraway over the ocean;**
　　　　　Pause far too long over the sea;
　　　　　Shit resolute motion on motion;
　　　　　Piss Coolies and Jews C.O.D.
　　　　　Pass cool jaw, you fool, spiel their bloody
　　　　　boloney
　　　　　While in a gaol cell far away, lonelier than
　　　　　lonely
　　　　　You, my boy, poor black boy, you and you and
　　　　　you only! . . . . .
　　　　　Oh bring back brave Barney to me!

L : 'Though labouring, the sun shines glistening dew
　　Through mist and moist over a thousand valleys
　　Pregnant between ten thousand hills in

147

> The province of birth from the sea
> Mist pouring beneficence
> Through groves of pineapples
> Plantations of sugar
> Sweet for all people
> Tropical breasts fruit
> Them all women
> The small women
> From over the sea
> Now native here
> Mildeyed
> Exiles
> Or tall
> Women
> Proud
> From the
> North
> Natal
> Gave
> Them
> Birth'

INT. 3 : **Even the wee men**

INT. 2 : **And the wee-wee menst —**

INT. 1 : **Stop it.**

INT. 2 : **'s true all I meant to say, was**

INT. 4 : **'Do you remember '49? Who murdered
A Bantu boy, till the Zulus fed the earth
With flames and the fat curdled
Milk of Indian profit and fear? Your girth
Is this brave country. Who herded
Proud cattle and warriors here from the
North?'**

L : 'Natal gave all birth.'

Ballad of the Cells

INT. 2 : **'Give him the works, the cheeky, stubborn bastard!'**

PULSE 17

NARRATOR: The writhing body's spasm shocks
    Barren conception of his life:
    Erect, impotent generation mocks
    The mind, the muscle's nervous strife.

    But out of these antitheses
    The spirit's contrapuntal theme
    Rises in rhythmic melodies
    Whose climax is the life of him,
    For unorgasmic ecstasies,
    Erect, indetumescent, climb.

L: That lovely old sun keeps breaking through
  A blessed thousand days and bays
    Urgent embracing capes, green inlets who
     Shell-scape this province of good hope
      Inside sweet waters, rain, sweet sea and dew
       Must pouring stills munificent
        In vineyards and orchards
         Of plums and sweet
          Dust blooming purple
           Slave seed and herdsman
            And hunters and exiles
             And dead hunters
              And the profuse
               Mixture of this
                Rich Cape of
                 Hope of
                  Various
                  'Life's
                   Long
                    Plenteous
                    Horn'

INT. 4: **'Ah ha! But where is Masilo now?**
And who is your giant in our old story?
Who is this heavenly Masilonyane?
Why has he, has he been given
The white cow?
We are sons of the same father?
In heaven yes! But
Masilonyane's is not all Africa
Do not cross the river
Looksmart, Ngudle, Masilo, my son,
Those who eat fish . . . .
They are your big brother
Who can evenly plough even the water.
They will eat with you, from your nation's
dish
And drink from your bowl,
Sitting round the rondavel,
The rebuilt lapa, here, here in our round hut.

L: Spiders moving along the wall,
Longlegged, weighing, waiting, dance;
Upon what innocent of ill
Filigree wing will fine silks pounce.

Feathers dust moistly underarm
In builded and fine angled art
To promise beds of coolth from harm
In web disturbed mind's hungry heart.

INT. 4: **When will your hand fashion your will?**

L: They swim. I sink and drink thick slime.

INT. 1: **What womb can prisoned loins 'compell'?**

L: She calls. I fall.

INT. 4: **'Now is the time!'**

NARR: Time is the gust of moving things,
Rhyming red rust on minute wings

Whose flight's fine as a feather sings:
Dead living dust like crystals, hair,
The burning lust of lungs for air
Turning, and yearning . . . time will bear.

Soft warmth sifts from life's muscled wave
And recreative sleep webs flesh:
Sweet life subtly suffuses limbs through meshed
Time's womb; dust proves deepest, osmotic love.

PULSE 18

NARR: Creative oceanic sleep is his;
Great walls, floors, turrets of his dreams
Glisten widely, clamour with bliss:
Day climbs, life builds, and teams and teems.

Rich, creamy udders tugged by young
Calves hungering for running love;
Gleaming machineries hum their deep, unending
    song
Of laughing labour's chugging drive

Below the chuckle of the hands,
Below care's cheerful tongue that proves,
Below the proving eyes that dance;
Above, . . . time's syncopating, breathing mind,

As coil on coil our deeds unwind
The shrouds around the dead romance
Until its murdered Looksmart moves
Rhythmic courage to symphonies
Of flowering desert and sweet seas —
The choral ONWARD of all lands.

PULSE 19

NARR: Pretoria's jacarandas wake!
Verandahless Cape-Dutch façades

151   F

Achelessly branch out purple, rak-
Ing claws through these Republican Volksraads

To level every irrigated rood
That laws have ploughed and M.P.'s sowed
With the quiescent and the urgent seed
That always flowers purple blood
The day interrogates the sun;
The sun beats violent flowers down
Until the violet middays run
Over Marabastad from the town.

PULSE 20

L: They dance confined in township, in
    The tourists' eye, to drum and flute:
    The song within my living skin
    Is penny-whistled, whispered, mute.

INT. 1: **What is your death to them?**

L: Death is compounded theirs in mine;
    Gold miners long for light and time
    While phthisis picks them, poking skew the long
    Lung's finite, infinitely fine rhythm.

PULSE 21

NARRATOR: The evening questions all his blood;
    Blood runs to faltering, nervous thrill;
    Young body's thrill is understood
    To undermine the bearded will.

PULSE 22

INT. 4: **What woman do you wish to have?**
    What quiet warmth? What mated sleep?
    Comradely whispering hands to bathe
    Your soul in pulsing musics, far and deep?
    African Samson, you lack love!

Ballad of the Cells

L (*and Woman's crooning voice*): Yes, soft and once again
  I hear your voice
   Delilah calling;
    Drifting through blinded brain
     It promises
      New blissful feeling
      Delilah . . . .
       My delightful!
      Delilah . . . .
       Peaceful bride, cool
       Cool
       Togetherness
      Of all exploring
        Hands
      Will unlock us,
      Oh! free
      Cramped, muscled feeling
      In our little deaths
      In all our deathless
       Dust.

L: Dust sand dry desert Gaza
  Dusty dusk over the sea
  Where the paper dry South Easter
  Day and duty blow away
  Where my dust storms dry the Karroo
  But the drought must also die
  When love rains from my disaster
  And when the spring grows gay.

  And all this time must stop
  When time will stay . . . .

INT. 2: **'God die bliksem is bedonnerd'**

L: Ineffable and away

INT. 2: **'Hy's stapelgek'**

INT. 3: **'Skoon van sy kop'**

153

INT. 4: **'All right, old chap. Call it a day'**

NARRATOR: Death may not be dishonour
Though it die, it die . . . . . . die day . . . . . .

L: Sweet death of day on kloof and bay;
Brave glowing rock and gleaming wave
Stay, distant . . . light, I come but sway . . . .
Stay . . . . . quiet . . . . . pain . . . . . or save me . . .
wave . . . .

Stay distant, light; and eyeless, day!

My death is not dishonour's prey.

PULSE 23

NARRATOR & L: Hands are not desperate that unlock
Imprisoned breath and fettered thought
Whose lonely echoing cell hollowly mock-
Ingly deride all that they, free, together, wrought.

L: Twin children have adopted love
And me to break the stammering walls
Of mourning, weeping, night:
A highstrung gemmed, frail woman's nerve
Streams telegrams of hope and calls
All men to morning's laughing light:

(*with children*) They call my name to manhood: 'Looksmart,
Look smart in the eye.' 'Look smart, Looksmart.'
And together: 'Looksmart, Look!
We stand with you in the brave heart
Of casteless, castled time.'

PULSE 24

NARRATOR: They took
His murder from the floor
And called a doctor: Closed the door.

The court must find that he has died.
Murder. Heart failure. Suicide . . .

PULSE 25

NARRATOR 1 : What verdict coroners of time?

NARRATOR 2 : What verdict corners of the world
Will point this mischief's vilest crime
That has the heart's fine leaves hard-furled?

NARRATOR 1 : Will antedate a tragic rhyme,
Fashion tongued love to chime, and chime
Changeless love's theme from clime to clime? —

NARRATOR 2 : Passion that's star-flung, flame-pure,
pearled!

NARRATOR DUO : Only your fisted anger now, sharp
wrath,
Can blaze the trail of Looksmart's path
To passion beautied beyond death.
Love's antidote to poisoned time.

PULSE 26

NARRATOR 2 : For when they draped
White shrouds around his raped
And brave but quiet heart,
No ghost escaped:
His spirit shaped
A song on the bloodless lips of dead Looksmart
On the smiling lips of his deathless heart:

PULSE 27

NARRATOR 1 : Listen
This entire land
Bands brothers
Mothers neighbours kin

In labours
All
Fire and joy

NARRATOR 2: And boy and girl
In spiral shell
And final pearl
Of bountiful
Growth
And beautiful
Fruit
Of truth

NARRATOR 1: Through structure and stricture
And number and function
To nimble factor and fracture
Facture
And section
And self
In life's wide flow
Waters' graceful
Democracy
And fire
Beyond
Distance
Of time and space
In starry
Knowledge
Throbs the race
Of living
Moving
Ocean
And
Animal
Man
Vegetable
Earth and motion
Man

And material
God is
Labour and love
In
Fashioning
Man
Finding
Him good
In the smile
Which we know is
Understanding
Beyond pain
And laughter
Beyond pleasure
And terror
And leisure
And beyond agony
Beyond
Ecstasy
Ecstasy
Which stands
Contemplative
Compassionate
Deedful
Needless
But for knowledge
And all love
And its sum
In the high sun
Some life
Life that is lovely
While love moves, and labour,
And then ripe ready all-ness,
When ripeness is all
Another ripeness is all
All is ripeness
And silent singing

Nor is my rest
Your silence
For alone
Even alone
Oh alone
For alone
Social Man
Living Man
Loving, labouring, smiling, rhythmical, muscular
Man

NARRATORS WITH L: Your hungry spirits
Always hungry spirits
Yearning
Haunted me
Nor will leave you
Alone . . . .

Overseas

MBELLA SONNE DIPOKO

Mbella Sonne Dipoko *was born in 1936 in Douala, Cameroon, but grew up in Western Cameroon and Nigeria. He joined the Nigerian Broadcasting Corporation in 1958 and became a News Reporter but has lived in France since 1960 and for a time studied law at Paris University. He has published two novels,* A Few Nights & Days *(AWS 82) and* Because of Women *(AWS 57), also a book of poetry,* Black & White in Love *(AWS 107). Dipoko's articles, short stories, and poems have appeared widely. His early poems were first broadcast by the BBC African Service which also produced* Overseas *in 1968.*

CHARACTERS

Ma Ndutu, *a village widow in her late fifties.*
Mbedi, *a literate young man.*
Mbongo, *a farmer, and his wife.*
Muledi, Mpanjo *and* Etondi, *African students in Europe.*
Ma Dikobo, *Muledi's aunt and Ma Ndutu's elder sister.*
Ndongo, *Muledi's fiancée, and her friend* Ewudu.
Jombwende, *Ndongo's aunt.*
A Canoeman.

SCENE ONE

*Late afternoon in an African village. Some of the huts lean
sideways supported from falling by forked posts. A few have
actually collapsed. Creeping weeds flourish on their roofs.
The sound of a cock beating his wings and then crowing.
People are talking in the distance. A mother calls.
A child answers. But we do not see them.
A hen and chicks cross the compound of a hut on the
verandah of which are* MA NDUTU, *an ageing woman,
and* MBEDI, *a young man. They are sitting on* bokuka
*stools. The young man has a letter in his hands.
Another cock crows. The atmosphere is one of waiting.*

MA NDUTU (*looking in pain, sad and calmly anxious*): Tell
me, my son, what does he say?

MBEDI: Mother, most of what he says is sad. I don't
even think I understand everything he says.

MA NDUTU (*slightly impatient*): You just tell me. Tell me
word after word. Even when he was here he had
his own way of speaking. He talked of love and of
death as if they were words in a dirge. Even when
he was still only a child he used to talk of the
evening as the return of the day and the night as
the promise. But the promise of what? That he
never explained. No one understood him; not even
his father, poor him, now lying in the cold earth
at the first turning of the road. His son must return
soon. His son must return. I shan't die until he has
returned; until both of us go to his father's grave,
on our lips the message of the living who love the
living and the dead.

MBEDI: But Ma Ndutu, you sound like him. You talk the
way he talks in this letter.

161

MA NDUTU: Then tell me what he says. Tell me word
after word. He is my son; And I remember his
first cries and his first dreams. He always dreamt
of the distance and longed to be away; but he wept
when the time came – the time to walk or to
voyage under the shadow of birds flying away. Yet
he would not hear of staying behind, always saying
he needed the sadness of departure in order to
know the joy of return.
Does he talk of return? Does he talk of the time
when birds brush their wings against the horizon
and fly back towards another afternoon, looking
like the clouds of the winds or like the waves of
the sea? Does he talk of such a day?

MBEDI (*eyes on the letter*): He says he thinks of you.

MA NDUTU: I always told him never to think too often
of me. I am the road along which he walked in
silence for nine months in the darkness of a forest
which will only be cleared with my life. (*sighs;
then her voice drops as she speaks more slowly*)
Sometimes there were storms, and lightning; and
sometimes I wept for a dead relative or during a
quarrel with his father. I know he heard my
crying and the fury of the storms. But the lightning
I'm sure he did not see for I was enough cover.
And I know he wasn't afraid when *I* was afraid –
I who, like his father, was already at the crossroads.
And I do not think he wept when I wept.

His first cries came when he arrived at the
meeting-place of yesterday and today and all was
unfamiliar. All was strange. He had seen the sun
and seen other faces; had heard other sounds other
than the beating of my heart; but in spite of the
darkness of the long night all had been safe; all
had been love in me. That I always knew he would
never forget – the safety and warmth of that long

journey; the long dream in the darkness of the
beginning and the many days of growth towards
the sunny and rainy crossroads of doubt. Maybe
that is why he thinks of me. I am the place of
arrival and departure; and in the heart, the place
of return.

MBEDI: He says he thinks of you because you are alone.
But you must know his father is not dead for he,
his son, is alive. What is dead is the laughter of
the beginning, and of the morning, now that the
afternoon is hot and as always rather silent while
the sun shimmers and the dragonflies and
butterflies and wasps of memory fly about harmless
in thoughts of yesterday, that is, thoughts of the
first days under the sky of two seasons . . . (*pause*)
In the evening wind, no group of birds on a mission
to dreamland; no birds raising calls of love in a
group and flying towards the south. Birds that fly
towards hopeland, soliloquizing of love without
looking back because of the urgency of the mission
and because the way is long, fly alone and fly very
high, seeking the shelter of the clouds; and few
would believe how restless the night had become,
packing and unpacking promises, fidgeting with
hopes.

MA NDUTU: He is talking about his youth. My son feels
his youth is over.
    In his last message he said he had gone away
hoping to learn to build better shelters for himself
and for others; but what he saw over there were
people building to shelter themselves, birds
roosting alone. And those who still had a mission
were not accessible. Read those last few lines again.

MBEDI: Birds that fly towards hopeland, soliloquizing of
love without looking back because of the urgency

of the mission and because the way is long, fly
alone and fly very high –

MA NDUTU (*raising her hand*): That is enough. Strange
that the sun still rises when the evening no longer
brings the sleep of former times.

SCENE TWO

A roadside hut in a cacao farm by a river. The farmer
MBONGO *and his wife, both of them old folk, are*
sitting on their verandah from which they can see the river.
A canoe is on the beach.
MBEDI *comes out of a bush path on our right. One end*
of his loin-cloth is raised and he has a stave in his right hand.

MBEDI (*walking into the compound*): How, did you see the
evening?

MBONGO and his WIFE: Yes . . .

WIFE: We saw the evening a bit. And you over there?

MBEDI: We too saw the evening a bit.

WIFE: Esadi?

MBEDI: She's well.

WIFE: Mwenen?

MBEDI: She's well.

MBONGO: My concubine Ndutu?*

MBEDI: Ma Ndutu's health is again worrying her.

WIFE: *Uweh*, Ndutu and her health! I don't know.
(*Shakes her head in commiseration.*) Really I don't know.

*It often happens with the coastal tribes of southern Cameroun that
an elderly man will refer to an elderly woman as 'my concubine' even
though they aren't lovers. It merely suggests affection and esteem.

MBEDI: It is sad. And then she's just received a very sad letter from Muledi.

WIFE: Has that man written?

MBEDI: Yes. A very sad letter indeed. I don't know what has happened to him in the West.

MBONGO: But when is he coming back?

MBEDI: Are you asking me?

WIFE: Some say he's become a little mad.

MBONGO (*rather indifferently*): I won't be surprised. All those books he's been reading since he was a little boy –

WIFE: Muledi? Those are heads! Extremely intelligent. Always passed all his exams. And what modesty! You wouldn't believe he was such an educated man.

MBONGO: But there was something which wasn't all right about his going to the West.

WIFE: Ndutu didn't like the idea at all. But Muledi wouldn't hear of giving it up. According to him he was only just beginning his studies.

MBONGO: Listen to that! Beginning his studies. When he had already finished all the big schools in Buea and Lagos . . .

WIFE: That was what he said. So to the West at all cost.

MBONGO (*to* MBEDI): But sit down awhile. Or are you in a great hurry?

MBEDI: Yes. I am following something ahead.

MBONGO (*with a wave of the hand*): Aa, go away, with your lies. Sit down. You are following something. What are you following?

MBEDI (*smiling and going to sit down on a stool*): You must have a calabash in there.

MBONGO (*mockly doubtful*): I don't know. I'll have to look. (*he rises and slightly bent, disappears into the dark doorway*) Maybe I have a cupful left. (*And then to his wife*) Your pot is burning.

WIFE (*springing up in near panic*): Uweh!
She too disappears into the hut. And then MBONGO *comes out with a calabash of palmwine and two cups.*

MBONGO (*sitting down*): They must ask Muledi to come back. Take. (*He hands* MBEDI *a cup*) What books is he still learning? (*pouring palmwine into* MBEDI's *cup*) It's five years now since he went away . . . *A*-woman.

WIFE: *E!*
MBEDI *tastes the palmwine.*

MBONGO (*now filling up his own cup*): It's five years now since Muledi is in the West, isn't it?

WIFE (*returning to the verandah and speaking in an emphatic tone of voice*): Yes. Njoe had just had her baby. And the child is five years old now. Yes. it's five years since he went away.

Silence. MBONGO *and* MBEDI *are drinking.*

MBONGO (*breaking the silence*): Books. Only God himself knows the kind of books he's still learning.

MBEDI: There's no end to books.

MBONGO (*brushing aside the remark with a wave of his left hand, as if unimpressed*): *Aa.* Let him come back and help his poor mother. Now that they have begun to say he's gone a little mad, it's time for him to be careful. No one should joke about the things said by the tongue that eats pepper and salt. He's been at

learning since the age of six. Yes, he was six when
his late father took him to Kumba. He finished
the school there. Then he went to Buea. He also
finished that one. And then to Lagos. And then
right to the West of the white people . . . *Bo-o!*
until he might end up growing old in books. *Aa*,
let him come back.

WIFE: And his intended Ndongo is already a big girl.

MBONGO: She's already a big woman. Do you think she's
going to wait for him? (*To* MBEDI): It's you people
who know how to read and write. Write to him.
Ask him to come back.

SCENE THREE

One week later. In MA NDUTU's *hut. Towards dawn.*
MA NDUTU *is in bed, moaning. Sitting by the bed and
watching over her is her elder sister,* MA DIKOBO,
*a kind old woman who has never been married in her life.
On the floor is an old lantern with a sooty globe. A log
fire is glowing in the centre of the room.*

MA DIKOBO: Glow, log fire, glow; glow to our eyes and
hearts. We wonder about the past and thoughts pick
their way through unmarked-out paths and our
beloved dead walk away in the night without
having left on our doorsteps the herbs to cure our
pains. And in our dreams we wait for their curative
advice, looking beyond the grave.
Talk, ancestors, talk; talk to us about those other
nights – streets paved with cowries and parcels of
your love that seems to have turned its back on us.

MA NDUTU (*moaning*): *Ate, ate, ate, uweh* . . .

MA DIKOBO: I cannot understand why you suddenly
became so ill again. Ndutu, I cannot understand.

Or is it the letter from Muledi that suddenly
worsened your health again? You worry too much
about him. Don't forget he's already a grown-up man.

MA NDUTU: It's not because of that letter. No, no.
Aye . . . I had begun feeling very ill when it
arrived. *Uweh, uweh* . . . .

MA DIKOBO: Where again are you feeling it now?
(*frowning*) I don't know why he's delaying. Where
again are you feeling the pain?

MA NDUTU: In the back. It begins, it begins, in the back.
Then it descends like a snake, biting away, to the
waist. Then it goes to the hip and then and then
to the thigh. No, it's not because of the letter.
Poor him, I don't know how he is tonight. In that
foreign land. I do not know whether or not he is well.
A young man should rejoice in the gifts of life
even when he thinks of the past; but with him
it's always sadness. (*sighs*) I do not know why he
ever went away. I do not like when he is sad. But
what can one do? Books, books, books. He's not
tired of books . . . *Uweh, uweh, uweh!*
He went to the shores beyond the ocean for the
beautiful seaweeds instead of paddling upstream to
the source of the river which is not far from here.
Books, books, books; what are books? The
wisdom of useless papers on which termites feed –
I really don't know . . . *Ate, aate* . . .

MA DIKOBO: Still in the back? Eh, where is the pain now?

MA NDUTU: In the leg. In the leg.

MA DIKOBO: I cannot understand the return of that fever
and pain. Three months ago your health was back
and your face was like a young woman's – eyes of
the evening and the night full of life and hope.

Who did not praise my lover's herbs? Not knowing the
pain had only gone into hiding. And I ask myself
why yesterday never keeps its promises. I ask
myself why hope cannot teach today and tomorrow
to dance the happy dances of ancient festivals.

MA NDUTU: It does. Hope teaches us what it can. Only,
only it still has to learn itself the ways of surprises
to which yesterday has nothing to say; for memories
speak only in the valley on the other side of the
hill of life. They do not know of hope. Memories
do not know the present nor tomorrow.
  Aate, ate, aaate . . .

MA DIKOBO: I know he'll cure you, the man to whose
place we'll be taking you tonight. Only I do not
know why that boy is delaying. I hope he arrives
in time for the tide.

MA NDUTU: What did I do? What did I do? I say what
did I do-*e*? E? E? E?
  *Outside the dawn is elbowing away the night and the
first cocks crow.*

MA DIKOBO: There they go, crowing, telling today and
tomorrow my sister is ill.
Crow, cocks, crow on; crow on our hopes. Soon
it will be the turn of partridges to remind us of our
youth and dawns of love;
Crow, cocks, crow on. Tell our ancestors the
other dawns delay when here there's still much work
to do. So let tomorrow and the other days to come
bring with them the strength of good health.

MA NDUTU: If it weren't because of him I wouldn't mind.
Uweh! When will he return? When? Home is
never everywhere and the heart once given to
sadness might think of the past as a place of no
joy. I want to see him married. His child. His

child. That is my wish. But I don't know. I do not
know. When he will return. And how far away he
is, my son, oh, how far away!

MA DIKOBO: Very far away, my poor sister. Far away
where no yodelling can reach; only the wind that
roams the world and returns and tells nothing
because it is dumb and blind.

MA NDUTU: The wind is dumb, but not blind. How
often have I seen it shaking branches as if trying
to tell me something about what it saw overseas!
No, no, no. The wind is not blind. It roams the
world wide-eyed as our thoughts of tomorrow.

MA DIKOBO (*going to light her pipe at the log fire*): The
wind is blind, my sister. The wind was blinded by
storms blowing birds and broken branches into its
wide eyes. (*Bends and takes a little ember with her bare
fingers; she puts it in the pipe and puffs away, returning
to the bedside.*) When the sky seems to groan it is
the wind moaning. (*sits down*) And it weeps
when it rains. Nor do you know for how long the
wind has been blinking at the blinding lightning.
For many years until it lost sight of the night and
the day . . . (*From behind the forest opposite the hut the
drunken voice of a canoeman is heard singing and swearing.*)
There he is, arriving at last. Drunk as he is, only God
knows how he's going to paddle that canoe tonight.

MA NDUTU: He'll paddle it all right. Why not? I'm
going to be treated by mermaids and there are
mermaids down the beach. They'll lead the canoe
to the south. Only I wish Mbedi were here. I
would have made him write a letter to his friend.
And my son's intended is away in the market. Is
everything ready?

MA DIKOBO (*takes away the pipe and spits in a corner*):
Yes, everything is ready. (*puts back the pipe in the corner of her mouth*) Now we are only waiting for that drunkard. I don't know why he decided to get drunk on a night like this.

MA NDUTU: He's still young. Don't forget that. Let him enjoy himself. We shall certainly arrive. There are mermaids in the river and our ancestors did not quarrel with those first inhabitants of the seas.

SCENE FOUR

Inside a hut. Night is falling. A pot is on a smoky fire. NDONGO, *a good looking girl of sixteen, is making the fire. Her friend,* EWUDU, *a much older girl in a fine print dress and even wearing shoes, is looking on.**

EWUDU: I'm telling you, you should come to Duala.

NDONGO: For a visit yes, just as I have been doing all this time. But I won't go and live there. I've told you my place is here until Muledi returns.

EWUDU: They say he's gone mad in the West.

NDONGO (*calmly*): It's not true. Ewudu, you know it's not true. He's well. If he seems mad it is only because he worries about us.
She shakes the firebrands and then blows against the embers.

MBEDI (*from outside*): Ndongo, *a*-Ndongo.

NDONGO: *E?*

MBEDI (*entering*): How, did you see the evening?

*See the poem 'Two Girls' in *Black and White in Love*, by the same author.

NDONGO: Yes. And you?

MBEDI (*standing by* EWUDU *and holding her head against his hip*): I didn't see the evening. (*He tenderly strokes* EWUDU's *face and then looks at her.*) So it's here you've been hiding? I've been looking for you all over the place. (EWUDU *looks up at him and smiles.*) Look at her face! (*to* NDONGO) Have you any news of Ma Ndutu?

NDONGO: They say she isn't getting any better. In fact her condition seems to be deteriorating.

MBEDI: Sometimes the years grow weak and cannot carry more days. Let her not die.

NDONGO: Don't say that again. That medicine man knows a lot. He'll certainly cure her.

MBEDI: Mermaid dances and a tall midnight woman in white under a cloudy sky that won't rain. Have you been there?

NDONGO: I am going there tonight. We'll be voyaging with the tide but stopping before the sea. They say she badly wants to see me.

EWUNDU: Then her condition is critical. It always is when ailing people on their sick beds ask to see this or the other person.

MBEDI: Yes. It's always ominious.

NDONGO: They say she's always asking for my intended. When would he arrive? When would he arrive?

MBEDI: Last month I read to her a letter he had sent. She said you were away visiting your sister.

NDONGO: She showed me the letter on my return. She said it was you who read it for her.

MBEDI: That day she said she wouldn't die until Muledi had returned. Have they written to him?

NDONGO: I hear his uncle doesn't want it. He says exams are approaching – the testing of memories of a thousand pages; and if he knew his mother was seriously ill that might disturb his studies of the wisdom of those parts.

MBEDI (*to* EWUDU): Let's go.

NDONGO: Wait and eat something. The food is almost ready. Sit down and eat something.

MBEDI: No. I am in a hurry. Tell them to write to him, or do it yourself. His return might revive her.

NDONGO: Where? Don't you know when a patient is asking for someone, seeing the person only hastens death? The satisfaction of a last wish makes the dying feel the struggle can now end.

MBEDI (*turning towards the door as* EWUDU *rises*): Is that why they won't tell him his own mother is dying? Tell them to write to him for the earth is about to open its doors once more and I hear his mother is already talking of the cold murmurings on lonely roads.

SCENE FIVE

Night on the river. Drums, miken and singing in the wind. The moon is in clouds. A few stars lighten the darkness. NDONGO *and her aunt* JOMBWENDE *appear in a canoe being paddled by a young man. Behind, far away, the solid outline of huge trees stunted in perspective. In front and on either side of the river, mangrove trees. And as if from the first bend downstream comes the persistent sound of the mermaid dance.*

CANOEMAN (*in a declamatory tone of voice*): Night on our
noble river wide and flowing like eternity in flood!
(*Pause. His paddle in his left hand, he cups the right and
takes water in it and drinks a couple of times after which
he resumes paddling.*) It was at this very spot two weeks
ago that Ma Ndutu raised all of a sudden such a
god of a shout; her sister stood up abruptly, asking
what had happened. The canoe swayed. Only
God helped we could have capsized.

JOMBWENDE: Why did she shout?

CANOEMAN: It was in a dream but she wouldn't tell us
what it was all about. *Beh!* Listen to those drums!
The sound of a force that cures. Who should see
him now with his hunch back, that sorcerer,
ushering in himself in the presence of his mermaid!
And like me he's paddling to the west of the sea.

JOMBWENDE: Sometimes I think the hospital would have
been better, for I have known cases of possessed
dancers beating a patient to death. So do not talk
only of curing. It is also a force that sometimes
kills while ghosts stand about breathless, and wizards
laugh not minding they too would die some day.

CANOEMAN: He talks to his mermaid about them all –
complaints of the sorcerer; and never mention the
hospital again, for there too people die and besides
the white man does not see in the night . . .
But why is Ndongo so silent? Are you thinking of
Muledi?

NDONGO: I am listening, wondering about the meaning
of our days.

CANOEMAN: They are all we have, our days, and once
they turn their backs on us there is no longer a
tomorrow or a yesterday . . . Listen to the joy of
those drums! It is hope.

JOMBWENDE: I do not know why the air feels so grisly.
I am afraid and as my daughter wondering about
the meaning of our life on earth.

CANOEMAN: Women, hope is the dawn. It is no longer
far away. I feel the morning star among the clouds.

SCENE SIX

*The following morning. A virtually dark room in the
medicine man's house.* NDONGO, JOMBWENDE *and*
MADIKOBO *are at the sick* MA NDUTU'S *bedside.*

NDONGO: Ma Ndutu, Ma Ndutu, remain on this side of
the day. We do not know what lies beyond our
farms and the river.

MA NDUTU: *E? e? (moaning and turning on her side in order
to face them)* How? Have you arrived?

NDONGO: Yes, Ma Ndutu.

MA NDUTU: Who is that with you?

JOMBWENDE: It's me, our mother. Get well in time. You
are being expected back in the village.

MA NDUTU: You also came? With whom did you leave
those children? They still aren't grown up, you
know; so be mindful.

JOMBWENDE: Their father is there, and their sister who
is no longer a child. That is why I came.

MA NDUTU: Thanks a lot. Thanks, for there isn't much
time left, my daughter.

NDONGO: There is. Mother of my intended, you must
be present at the wedding.

MA NDUTU: No, *aate,* no. There isn't much time left.
(She takes NDONGO's *hand in hers and moves a bit,*

*turning to lie on her back. All the time she's moaning
because she is in pain.*) Have you written to him?

NDONGO: Yes, Ma Ndutu. He knows by now, unless of
course the message was delayed.

MA NDUTU: Is it long since the man-made bird flew to
him with your message on its wings?

NDONGO: Six days ago. It was on the last market day.

MA NDUTU: Write to him again. Write to him for the
hooting of the owls becomes more and more
persistent and they do not hoot of hope; and the
cats are crying already. Yes, write to him. Tell him
I am going to meet his father. Tell him never to
lose hope in tomorrow not even when the river
rises on a beach without canoes. Let him wake up
in the morning and sleep at night and not remain
awake at night and sleep in the morning . . . Life
is short and we do not know what lies beyond.
Maybe only darkness or simply the earth which is
neither hot nor cold, for dead bodies do not feel;
skeletons do not hear or see. (*shaking her head*) I do
not know. Tell him I say all that because of his
last letter. He must make the journey as happy as
possible. Otherwise like birds you will fly towards
us – we the dying and the dead, never singing, only
crying, regretting life and happiness, all very good
things, which is why we die in pain; and those
who die, smiles on their faces only lie, and it is a
sad thing to lie and even worse to lie at the hour of
goodbye. (NDONGO *and her aunt are sobbing softly,
wiping their eyes with the backs of their hands.*) Don't
cry. Why are you crying?

SCENE SEVEN

MULEDI *and an African girl* ETONDI *and her fiancé*
MPANJO *are in a room on a high floor. A record is on*

*an electrophone standing on the floor – concerto for flute
and orchestra. Through the french window on our right we
see the roof of a European city. The sky is blue. The
walls of the room are lined with bookshelves.* MULEDI *gets
up and goes to tune the music even lower.*

MPANJO: *Uweh*, home!

ETONDI (*to* MULEDI): Will you go?

MULEDI (*returning to his seat*): Yes. I feel I have to be
with them. To work with them. They must learn
to be happy again. I'm going home. What am I
doing here?

MPANJO: But you haven't taken your doctorate.

MULEDI: What is a doctorate? My mind is made up. I
am going home. I have to organize the happiness
into which my children will be born. The family
is everything. And learning without happiness is
futile. It is time for me to enlarge the family. Time
I began having children of my own – harvesters of
our dreams. My intended is waiting for me.

ETONDI: Do you still hear from Ndongo?

MULEDI: It was she who wrote to me about it. (*pointing*)
That's her letter on the table. (*He gets up again and
reaches for the letter; looks through its pages and detaches
the last two which he hands* ETONDI.) Read from there.
(*She begins to read to herself.*) Read it aloud so that
Mpanjo may also hear.

ETONDI (*reading slowly*): Yes, that was how your mother
died two days after that visit to her. News of her
death preceded the body by half a day and I sat
out alone all night. It was cold and the moon very
bright while in the distance dogs barked a lot.
Then towards dawn the moon turned round a

corner in the sky and disappeared behind a hill of
clouds and I heard voices break out on the beach,
weeping, crying, calling you; and I knew they had
brought your mother's body. People came out of
their houses and soon all the women of the village
were crying. Clouds had moved up in the low sky
where only a star shone like a torch to light your
way back to all our suffering and our waiting . . .
To all our suffering and our waiting. (*sighs*) Write
to me. Write soon before the first weeds sprout on
her grave which is near your father's.

MPANJO: By God, life is sad!

ETONDI (*to* MULEDI): Have you replied?

MULEDI (*nods, rising and going to look out of the window, his
hands clasped behind him*): Yes I have written to her
to tell her that I'll be flying home as soon as possible
to weep on those thirsty graves, wetting that parcel
of land with my tears. And that would be the last
time I should ever weep. (*turns round to face them*)
For the rest of the land we shall water with our
sweat and then we shall replant the dream . . .

MPANJO (*musingly*): Replant the dream!

MULEDI: Yes, *a*-Mpanjo. Her death has reminded me of the
urgency of the mission and I refuse at once despair
and hope both being only a kind of waiting which
we can no longer afford never having enough years
with which to pay for wasted time; and there is the
end – death in which we lose all our breath and
our life and become nothing but memories of
burials and tears.

CURTAIN *from behind which as the audience begins to
rise,* ETONDI *is heard reading* NDONGO's *letter all over
again.*

ETONDI'S VOICE: Yes that was how your mother died two days after that visit to her. News of her death preceded the body by half a day and I sat out alone all night. It was cold and the moon very bright while in the distance dogs barked a lot. Then towards dawn the moon turned round a corner in the sky and disappeared behind a hill of clouds and I heard voices break out on the beach, weeping, crying, calling you; and I knew they had brought your mother's body. People came out of their houses and soon all the women of the village were crying. Clouds had moved up in the low sky where only a star shone like a torch to light your way back to all our suffering and our waiting . . . .

THE END

THE END

This Time Tomorrow

NGUGI WA THIONG'O

Ngugi Wa Thiong'o (*James Ngugi*) *was born at Limuru in 1938 and was educated in Kenya and at University College Makerere where he wrote* Weep Not, Child *and* The River Between. *And then whilst at the University of Leeds he wrote* A Grain of Wheat. *He has also published a play,* The Black Hermit *in African Writers Series. He is now a Lecturer at the University of Nairobi. Previously he lectured at Makerere and then spent a year at Northwestern University, Illinois attached to the Program of African Studies.* This Time Tomorrow, *with two other plays by this author, has also been published in Kenya by the East African Literature Bureau.*

181

CHARACTERS

Journalist
Editor
Njango, *A very poor, middle-aged woman*
Wanjiro, *Her daughter*
3 Customers
Inspector Kiongo, *A municipal health officer*
Tinsmith
Shoemaker
Asinjo, *A young taxi driver, Wanjiro's boyfriend*
Stranger, *A dedicated and active analyst and prophet*
Police Officer
Crowd and Policemen

This Time Tomorrow

A journalist is furiously typing at one corner of the stage. The spotlight should pick him out while the rest of the stage remains dark.

VOICE: Hey! Hey man!
The journalist stops, listens. The voice (of the editor) continues.

EDITOR: Hurry up! The whole bloody paper is hung up while we wait for that article of yours!
The journalist resumes typing. Then he stops with a triumphant full stop and rips the sheet out of the machine.

JOURNALIST (*to himself*): There! It's finished. This could be the best thing I've ever done. The Sunday feature to end all Sunday features. Let's see how it reads: 'The filthy mushrooms – inhabited by human beings – besieging our capital city, came tumbling down yesterday. Wading . . .' – no, groping, I think – '*Groping* through clouds of dust and smoke, the City Council warriors, with their scythes, sickles and batons, hacked left and right. Rotting tins flew high in the air. The cardboard walls and the dry mud squeaked, wobbled, and then crashed.' H'm, not bad. 'Suddenly, one was back in the days of Joshua, when the legendary walls of Jericho come tumbling down. Clean-the-City campaign had started. Your reporter, who at no time left the demolition line, brings you a minute-to-minute, eye-witness account of those drama-packed, tension-ridden hours before the mighty collapse at noon. 'It was in the small hours of the morning that I reluctantly disengaged myself from bed, dipped my head in water, and then with my camera and a notebook, sped towards the shanty-town near the country bus terminus. Not a human soul was in sight. The terminus, normally full of beehive activity, was now as quiet as the Kalahari or Sahara desert.

I could not see the disorderly rows and rows of shanty slums, because it was so dark. But soon, I could just discern a few intermittent voices rising out of the smell and the darkness:'

Meanwhile, i.e. during the last half of his narrative, dawn-light reveals the inside of Njango's shelter made of cardboard and rotting tin. The shelter should be suggested by a small wall which can be quickly removed or retained depending on the need of the action. The rest of the stage is a slum yard (with suggestion of similar shelters). Njango and Wanjiro share the floor as bed – just beside the small wall.

NJANGO: Wanjiro! Wanjiro! (*Wanjiro snores*) Wake up! Wake up! I tell you! (*Wanjiro goes on snoring*) What a heavy load of flesh! This brat will surely kill me. Other girls rise up before the sun to help with morning chores. (*Wanjiro snores*) This one snores like a pig. I will truly pinch your fat nose or drench your face with cold water. Wake up!

WANJIRO (*in sleepy fright*): What – what – water? Who is talking of water? (*yawns with sleep*) I had such dreams. (*excitedly*) Water everywhere.
Floods and floods that destroyed and washed away these slums —

NJANGO (*impatiently*): You dwell in dreams. When will you wake up? Customers will soon be here. Githua, Macharia, Gitina and the others. We must cook this meat. We must make something drinkable from yesterday's bones.

WANJIRO: Bones, decaying meat, white maggots, tins, paper, broken pots – all these were carried away. And fleas bloated with blood to the size of rams – I saw them ride high on the waves. Then they drowned.

NJANGO: What are you talking about?

WANJIRO: The water – the floods that carried away these shacks.

NJANGO (*sighing reminiscently*): You always dream of flames. Yet you were so young. Two or three years. You slept all the night – as if you were dead. Yes, you slept God's sleep as they burnt down our house. That was in the country. The blood-flames leapt to the sky. A shiver went through my bones, but I could not cry. We sheltered under the roof of the latrines. Dawn found us there. It was the colour of the earth. Then you woke up, and you cried for food. And your brother cried for food, and I had nothing to give. (*bitterly*) Nothing.

WANJIRO: It was water, mother. Last night it was really water.

NJANGO: You should have drowned in it. You and your dreams! Put on your clothes quickly. I want you to sweep the floor while I go to make fire in the compound. Sweep it well, now! (*goes out into the yard to split wood*)

WANJIRO (*dully*): Yes, mother.
Sweeping. Wanjiro grunts and breathes heavily.

WANJIRO (*sneezing*): This dust will kill me! (*sneezes again. As she sweeps she hums a tune. Suddenly she gives a little scream as she bumps into the doorpost*) Oh! The door again. My head will surely split in two. Oh, oh. My mother is right. My dreaming and singing will, in the end, be my death. (*breathes deeply. It turns into a sigh*) How often have I leaned against this very post, and watched the city awake. Just now, noise is dead in the city. It is so dark outside – the crawling maggots in the drains are hidden. (*breathes deeply again*) The stench of human urine – Lord! *Njango, who has been splitting wood with an axe, now starts to make a fire.*

WANJIRO: And my mother at work again – breaking
wood, striking a match. Presently there will be a
roaring fire. Familiar scenes – familiar sounds. I
am tired of them.
Njango lights the fire.

WANJIRO: See, see! Once again she has lit up the sky!
Soon now follows the light of day. I don't like the
sun. It always increases the smell in this place.
(*sighs*) Why is it that I never saw these things before
I heard the stranger speak? His eyes were so deep,
and powerful . . . Asinjo has eyes like the stranger. I
wish my mother had not driven Asinjo away . . .

*Pause. Cocks crow, babies cry and tins clash as more slum-
dwellers wake up. Njango is placing a pot (for making
soup) on the fire, adding water to it as the journalist
continues with his narration.*

JOURNALIST: 'Soon, cocks started crowing. From where I
stood, I could hear babies crying, and the occasional
clashing of tins. There were more voices now. The
village was waking up. It was blowing cold. I was
shivering. But I stuck firmly to my post. I knew
something – some news – would come my way. I
could hear it in the voices . . .'

WANJIRO: The village is waking up. Yet the birds are
hardly awake.

NJANGO (*coming back*): You want to imitate the birds, do
you, Wanjiro? Remember birds don't have to kill
themselves in order to live. And do they need
money to buy food? No. Do they have to buy
clothes and pay school fees for little brats like you
and your brother? No. Take away that rubbish to
the drain. Have you not yet sorted out the bones?

186

WANJIRO: Mother, you mock me with your talk of clothes and school. Where is my brother? You sent him to my uncle in the country so that he might attend school. Me, you kept here to work for you. Where are the clothes you buy me? Look at other girls in this place. They wear clean frocks on Saturdays and Sundays. I am ashamed to walk in the streets.

NJANGO: You speak to me like that? Do you know who I am? Do you? I will tell you. My aged loins heaved you forth into this world. You were so tiny and sickly. Oh, I should have kept a baby's boot, like the Masai do. Then you could look at yourself sixteen years ago. You cried at night, and Lord, how many nights and days did I go without sleep!

WANJIRO: You always silence me with such talk. That is how you persuaded me to forget Asinjo. I never asked to be born.

NJANGO (*ignoring her*): And your father would not help. Just sat there with other men from the ridge, taking snuff and talking about the stolen land. Sometimes they sang and laughed. Then the old man came from the land of the white people . . . And the songs and the laughter were no longer the same . . . Their eyes became hard and set. (*stirring herself from the past*) Lord, how I have laboured for these ungrateful wretches. And now she talks to me with a haughty tongue. What do you think Asinjo would have done for you? Just what do you think Asinjo would have done for you?

WANJIRO: He would have taken me away from this place.

NJANGO: You would have been lost in the city.

WANJIRO: Asinjo would have protected me.

NJANGO: Protected you? A man of another tribe? Do you know what men are in this city? Have you not heard of women left in the gutter? Women stabbed and left to die in the streets? Protect you! I am glad the wretch has for ever vanished from my sight.

WANJIRO: He had such deep eyes.

NJANGO: And such thick lips – as big as a mountain.

WANJIRO (*tenderly*): A smooth skin.

NJANGO: So black – blacker than the soot on that pot.

WANJIRO: I wish he would come back for me. Our village will be destroyed today.

NJANGO: Let me never hear you say that again. Come for you? Asinjo come into my household? Good Lord! Have I fed you, given you clothes, undergone all this suffering so that you would be wasted on a man from another tribe?

WANJIRO (*relenting a little*): I know how much you have suffered in this city. You have fought with drunks, wrestled with wolves and hyenas in this Uhuru Market. I've never wanted to disobey you . . . Two days ago I saw a dress in the city. I wanted it so much, I almost stole it.

NJANGO: You want to dress like white people?

WANJIRO: Black people wear clothes like those I saw.

NJANGO: This city is not for us.

WANJIRO: The stranger says the city belongs to us. The shops, the factories, everything.

NJANGO: Alas, only to a chosen few.

WANJIRO: The poor peasants and workers, who fought for Uhuru shall inherit this earth, he says.

NJANGO: Who is this stranger? He is a cheat and a loafer.

WANJIRO: But mother, he led a delegation to the City Council! He is not a man with ambitions. He has no bad designs on the people of this village. He always keeps to himself. He was reluctant to lead the delegation to the Council.

NJANGO: Why did he do it, then?

WANJIRO: The men showed him the notice – we had only been given a few days to move away. And don't you remember how women wept in front of him, before he agreed to write their letter and lead the delegation? And you call him a cheat and a loafer! It is so unfair, mother!

NJANGO: What good did that delegation do us, what good?

WANJIRO: His tongue made the City Council give us a few months of grace.

NJANGO: City Council or no City Council, I am not moving from this place.

WANJIRO: Some people say he works in magic.

NJANGO: He is only a trouble-maker. Go out and put these bones into the pot.

WANJIRO: Yes, mother.
Njango hums or sings a tune as she too puts pieces of meat into the pot.

WANJIRO: Mother!

NJANGO: Yes!

WANJIRO: Have you decided what you are going to do?

NJANGO: What do you mean?

WANJIRO: Outside, everybody is talking about today's demonstration. Are we going to meekly pull down our house with these, our hands, or shall we fight?

NJANGO: Stop chattering and help me here. Quick. This is not the old City Council. But old or new, I am not pulling down my house, do you hear? Hold the meat properly while I cut!

WANJIRO: I am afraid – you might chop my fingers.

NJANGO: Don't be foolish. How many times have I chopped your fingers off? There! Stop shaking the meat!

WANJIRO: Mother!

NJANGO: You never give me a moment's peace, do you? What do you want to ask? Not about your City Council, I hope?

WANJIRO: Have you met him?

NJANGO: Who?

WANJIRO: The stranger.

NJANGO: He just wants to get us into trouble. I never attend his silly meetings.

WANJIRO: He worked long for the white man. Then he went to detention. When he came back his little piece of land had been taken away. He says he will hew and carry wood no more.

NJANGO: Listen – you must not see him again.

WANJIRO: Why?

NJANGO: I can't explain. Oh, you are still a child.

WANJIRO: Before I heard the stranger, yes. I was ignorant. I knew no world beyond these slums.

NJANGO: He is dangerous. Do you hear me? He is dangerous . . . Your father used to talk like that.

WANJIRO: What happened to my father? You always keep
silent whenever I ask you about him. You only
stare into space and your eyes cloud with unshed
tears.

NJANGO: He was my man – strong, sure, but troubled.
Like the other men in the land he, too, foolishly
cried defiance to the white man. He went to the
forest. Dedon Kimathi led them, and for many
years they fought against the bombs and guns in the
mountains and the forests. One day reports reached
us. Your father was captured. They shot him dead
like a dog. (*silence, then quietly*) What has this Uhuru
brought us? Brought to us who lost our sons and
husbands?

*Cock crowing; chickens cackling. As the journalist resumes
his narrative, Njango and Wanjiro put out a table and
mugs (calabashes) and generally prepare for the customers
who will soon be coming for a morning mug of soup.*

JOURNALIST: 'And so, daylight broke. The morn, in
russet mantle clad, walked o'er the dews of those
disorderly slums. The incessant din of human voices
rose to a drowning crescendo. It was another House
of Babel. Tinsmiths were beating their tins. Fleets
of buses from the country vomited out people who
streamed away in every direction, like disturbed
safari ants. Most wallowed into the shanty town for
their morning cup of soup. The sound of sizzling
meat placed me in a state of hunger. I followed the
streams of men into the slum town, and mingled
with the populace. The tantalizing smell of meat!
I rushed with the others for a morning cup of
soup . . .'
Journalist goes out during this bit of action.

1ST CUSTOMER: Njango – mother of men!

2ND CUSTOMER: Our daily bread! Give us this day our daily bread!

3RD CUSTOMER: And forgive us our sins. We are late for our morning soup.
Njango dishes out the soup, at the same time crying out in competition with other sellers advertising their wares.

NJANGO: Soup for twenty cents. Soup for twenty cents. Soup to build your bones!

NJANGO
WANJIRO } *(together)*: Soup is cheap here today.

1ST CUSTOMER: Soup cheap! Soup cheap today! It is always twenty cents!

2ND CUSTOMER: Njango, you old whore, you know how to milk your men!

3RD CUSTOMER: Give me another mug of soup. You have got to be taught to live in this market city.

NJANGO: ⎫ Soup for twenty cents. Soup to build your
WANJIRO: ⎭ bones!
Enter Inspector Kiongo speaking from a loudspeaker.

KIONGO: This is the voice of the City Council. This is the voice of the City Council, calling on all those that dwell in Uhuru Market.

1ST CUSTOMER: Good God! Of course, today is the day!

2ND CUSTOMER: What are we to do?

3RD CUSTOMER: Let us hear what the madman has to say.

KIONGO: This is Inspector Kiongo of the City Council Health Department. I remind all those that dwell in these places that today was the date I gave your last delegation. A month is now over. By twelve o'clock today these shacks must be demolished. They are a great shame on our city. Tourists from America, Britain, and West Germany are disgusted with the dirt that is slowly creeping into a city that used to be the pearl of Africa.

1ST CUSTOMER: They cannot destroy our homes.

2ND CUSTOMER: I didn't know they were so determined to punish us.

3RD CUSTOMER: Is this not a black man's government – *our* government?

KIONGO: Clean-the-City Campaign begins today.

People murmur angrily. Meanwhile the journalist enters with camera and notebook. He is taking pictures left and right, and interviewing people. Kiongo poses for a picture.

JOURNALIST (*to tinsmith*): You, sir! You! I am a newspaper reporter. I want to get your angle on the story – how you feel about this move, and so on and so forth. Hold it! Hold it! I want to take your picture. There! Now, what is your trade?

TINSMITH: I am a tinsmith.

JOURNALIST: How old?

TINSMITH: Age? Fifty, sixty, I cannot say.

JOURNALIST: When did you come into this city?

TINSMITH: When? Let me count – one, two, three, oh, many years ago.

JOURNALIST: What occupation had you, before you came here?

TINSMITH: I have done many jobs, cooking, washing, sweeping. I was a cook. That is, I cooked for white

people during the war and after. Even today, few
black people eat the kind of things I can cook. I
lived in the Rift Valley for a time, as a cook and a
squatter. Was driven out during the emergency.
Once I worked as a porter – with the Railways
and Harbours. That's a fine job, in a way. Sometimes they would give you a tip – a shilling or two.
That was good – you had something to eat. But
afterwards there was nowhere to lie down. You slept
on shop-verandahs, in trenches, anywhere. Once or
twice I slept in public latrines. Phew! The smell!
Then I worked – let me see, my memory fails me. I
remember moving from place to place, from job to
job, driven on by police and hunger. They let me
have no peace anywhere. That is to say, none until I
found a place in this market. I learnt my trade. And
now I make water-tins, pangas, jembes, braziers –
anything – anything . . .

KIONGO: Good people! Remember, this is your city. Be
proud of it and keep it clean.

NJANGO: Puuu. His voice makes me spit. What a tongue!
Is that not Kiongo! He used to come here – every
lunch time. A bowl of soup and a fleshy bone, and
he would go away all thanks and gratitude. A
member of the Youth Wing, he was, in those days,
and he used to whimper with hunger. Now he is a
King – a King!

KIONGO: Remember our Prime Minister. He told idlers,
beggars, harlots, and the jobless who flock to the
city: Go back to the land.

Angry murmurs.

JOURNALIST (*to shoemaker*): I am a newspaper reporter. I
want to get your angle on the story. How do you
feel about this move, and so on and so forth. Keep

194

still. No! Look a bit angry! Raise that stick in a threatening manner. You know, as if you are going to fight the City Council. There! That will make a magnificent photo. Now, what is your trade?

SHOEMAKER: I am a shoemaker.

JOURNALIST: Age?

SHOEMAKER: I don't know my age.

JOURNALIST: You are married?

SHOEMAKER: I've one wife and five children. They live here with me.

JOURNALIST: What do you feel about this rather provocative action by the City Council?

SHOEMAKER: It is not that I don't want to move. But the government should give me a place to go to. After all, I deserve it. I was a member of the Party – an active member, you might say. I took the oath in 1950. I felt a new man. Who did not? I mean, of those who took the oath? We were fighting for freedom. We were fighting for our soil. We used to sing: 'Even if they deride me, and beat me and kill me,
They shall never make me forget,
This is a black man's country.' I was arrested and sent to Manyani. Manyani – you have not heard of it? A concentration camp. See? I came home after the emergency. The whiteman had not gone. No job for me, no land either. So I came to this city. No, no, I will not talk about what I saw here. Just this: I've been doing fine. Mending a shoe here and there. That is, I have not starved. Tell me, tell me good people – why then should I move from here?

KIONGO: Clean-the-City Campaign starts today. At twelve today. At twelve o'clock, the police will act. Show the Harambee spirit, and move! (*goes out, followed by the journalist, who wants to interview him*)

NJANGO: I never heard such cheek. Show the Harambee spirit by destroying our homes?

TINSMITH: I only wanted to be left alone.

SHOEMAKER: What can I do? I've no more strength to defend my own.

1ST CUSTOMER: Why don't we hold a meeting with the stranger? He works in magic. Will he not blind their eyes?

2ND CUSTOMER: Yes. The stranger's magic will save us.

ALL: A meeting! A meeting! Everybody – to the meeting at once! Long live Uhuru Market. Long live Uhuru Market. (*go out*)

NJANGO: Wanjiro – I too am going to the meeting to hear the stranger. Look after that soup and meat until I come back. (*exit*)

WANJIRO (*sighing*): So they think the stranger will help them. I don't want to go. I don't want the stranger to work his magic. I want to get out of here, out of these slums. Look at me. I don't have clothes like other girls. I am now a woman. Yet no man dares glance in my direction.
Well, maybe once or twice, but only to ask: Who is that thing in rags? Asinjo was different though. Used to touch my breasts. He even said I was beautiful. I felt such joy – the first time. I could not believe it. I ran to a glass window in the city, and looked at my own reflection. Not bad really. There was something in the face —

ASINJO (*in a whisper*): Wanjiro! Wanjiro!

WANJIRO: Asinjo! Is it really you?

ASINJO: Can I come in? Is your mother there?

WANJIRO: She has gone to the meeting. Come.
Quickly. Would you like some soup?

ASINJO: Yes – it is a bit cold today. Here, take this.
(*rustles paper money*)

WANJIRO: Ten shillings! Oh, where have you got so much
money? You don't have to pay, though.

ASINJO (*impatiently*): I am no longer without a job. I am
a taxi-driver.

WANJIRO (*clapping her hands for joy*): A taxi – you mean you
actually drive?

ASINJO: Yes. Now I know every part of the city. From
Kolo, where Europeans live, to Westlands and
Kabete, where rich Africans have bought stone
houses. Would you like a ride through the city?

WANJIRO: Oh Asinjo! I would like that very much. But –
my mother!

ASINJO: 'My mother! My mother!' You are not a child
any longer. You can't let an old woman go on
shutting you away from the good things of life!
When I used to come here, she drove me away with
her wild tongue. Said that I was jobless, that I was
not of your tribe. What does that matter? I have
now got a good job, and many girls want me. If
I did not love you, would I have come back after
all the names your mother called me? Would I?
(*silence*) You say nothing. Then come with me.
Your mother is only an old woman who doesn't
know the ways of the world, or the needs of a young
woman. Besides, these slums will be destroyed today. Where will you go? I've got a house now in
Old Jerusalem. Come with me! You'll cook for me,

keep the house clean, and I'll buy you nice dresses
and shoes and . . .

WANJIRO: Oh Asinjo – I love you so much! Just now, I
was thinking of you, and how you used to touch my
breasts, and I almost wept . . . But this is too sudden!

ASINJO: It is never too soon to have a good life. Please
come with me.

WANJIRO: My mother is all alone, Asinjo.

ASINJO: We can come and see her sometimes. And bring
her presents.

WANJIRO: Give me time to think about it. Where is your
taxi?

ASINJO: At the Country Bus stop.

WANJIRO: Wait for me there. My mother will soon be
here.
I'll come and tell you of my decision.

ASINJO (*as he is going*): Yes. And come with all your
things!

WANJIRO: Good-bye, Asinjo! . . . oh yes, I long for the
pleasures of this glittering city. I want a frock. And
shoes – high heels – so that I can walk like a
European lady. A bag hanging from my left elbow –
fingering a cigarette in my right hand . . . (*goes out
walking like a European lady*)
Pause.

*The demonstrating crowd enters the stage chanting slogans
and carrying badly written posters. They sit down cheer-
ing and clapping and then fall to silence as the stranger
resumes his speech.*

STRANGER: Yes, I, the stranger among you, I was one of

those who fought for Uhuru in the forests and in the detention camps. But what has this Uhuru brought us?

CROWD: Nothing. It has brought us nothing!

STRANGER: Not nothing! It has brought us people who love driving Mercedes Benz, and long American cars! While we starve in the slums! Let the City Council leave us alone in our slums and our misery!

CROWD: Long live the stranger! Long live our houses!

STRANGER: I don't want to speak for long. But I want to say this: I don't work magic. I have not the powers of a witch-doctor. I cannot blind the eyes of a determined City Council.

CROWD: What is he saying? Why does he say this? He can help us? He *must* help us!

STRANGER: But there *is* magic! The magic is within you. The witchcraft with which to blind the City Council is within our hearts, in our hands. Let us stand together. Let us, with one voice, tell the new government: We want our homes, we love them. Unless the City Council shows us another place to go, where we can earn our bread, we shall not lift a finger to demolish our homes! I go further: we must defend our own!

CROWD: Long live Uhuru Market! Long live Uhuru Market!

1ST CUSTOMER: I don't like this kind of talk.

2ND CUSTOMER: I think he speaks well.

3RD CUSTOMER: It is true what he says. We must all stand together.

1ST CUSTOMER: Listen – the stranger is speaking again.

STRANGER: Friends, remember how we fought the white man! How so many of our sons and daughters withered away in detention camps, and in the forests. We fought for land! But where is the land?

CROWD: The white man has got it! Yes, the white man has got it!

STRANGER: We fought for Uhuru, because we were told it would mean decent houses, and decent jobs! But where are the jobs? Where are the houses?

CROWD: Not here! Not here!
Police siren approaching.

1ST CUSTOMER: Police! The police are coming!

2ND CUSTOMER: Run! Run quickly! Out of my way!

3RD CUSTOMER: But we should stand firm! The stranger said . . .

STRANGER: Brothers and sisters! I beseech you not to run away! Your cause is just! Your homes are dear to you!

1ST CUSTOMER: Watch out – they've got batons! Watch out!

3RD CUSTOMER: Stay, brother, stay!

2ND CUSTOMER: No, no! Let me go. Let me go!

STRANGER: Our people . . . our people . . . our people. . .

Police storm in hitting people with batons, people scream, shout, as they fight to get away.

POLICE OFFICER: I am a police officer. In the name of our new Republic, you are arrested for inciting a crowd to violence and civil disobedience! Follow us!

STRANGER (*last despairing appeal*): Friends!

CROWD *makes sullen mutterings which fade into silence.*

POLICE OFFICER: Come! Take him away, men!

> *Silence in the market. Then Wanjiro enters, still walking like a European lady. Soon Njango enters. But it is obvious that both are engrossed in their different worlds.*

NJANGO: So they have arrested the stranger. We have no leader. His eyes made me think of my man. Before he went to fight in the forest. Eyes fixed at nothing, and yet everywhere. He made me afraid, afraid I know not of what. Where will Wanjiro and I go when they drive us from here? Where to set up a new trade to earn us bread and water? Wanjiro!

WANJIRO (*approaching*): Yes, mother!

NJANGO: Have you sold more soup?

WANJIRO: Not much. Most people were at the meeting.

NJANGO: They have arrested the stranger.

WANJIRO: What! Arrested him?

KIONGO (*loudspeaker voice*): Hurry up! Hurry up! Take out all your things from the huts! The police will **not** touch them!

(Bulldozer noises throughout following scene.)

WANJIRO: Mother, I want to tell you something.

NJANGO: What?

WANJIRO: I am – I want to go away.

NJANGO: My poor child, we are all going away!

201

WANJIRO: Yes, mother. But I am not coming with you.

NJANGO (*suspicious*): How do you mean – not coming with me?

WANJIRO: I am going with Asinjo. He came for me while you were away.

NJANGO: With that man? A man of another tribe? A man without a job?

WANJIRO: He has got a job now. And a house in Old Jerusalem.

NJANGO: You must be off your head. I've told you about men of the city.

WANJIRO: Asinjo is different.

NJANGO: Different? Let me never hear his name on your lips again!

WANJIRO: I am going with him, anyway! You are old. You don't know the ways of the world, or the needs of a young woman.

NJANGO: No child of mine, from my own flesh, will sell her body. I'll break her bones, else she breaks mine first.

WANJIRO: I am old enough to look after myself. I am going now. Asinjo is waiting for me. Goodbye, mother.

NJANGO: Wanjiro! Wanjiro! Don't go away. Don't leave me alone! What shall I do without you? (*silence, then quietly*) I am a useless old woman.
Kiongo enters. But Njango does not hear him.

KIONGO: Hurry up! Hurry up! You there! Woman! What are you doing! Hurry up! (*runs out still shouting orders*)

NJANGO: They are herding us out like cattle. Where shall I go now, tonight? Where shall I be, this time tomorrow? If only we had stood up against them! If only we could stand together!

Then bulldozer whine to crescendo, and resultant crash as hut is pushed down. Then silence.

CURTAIN

Episodes of
an Easter Rising

DAVID LYTTON

David Lytton *was born in South Africa where he spent
his first 21 years; he left in 1948 when the Nationalist
government came into power. He has lived in the United
Kingdom since then, mainly at Stratford upon Avon.
He is a stage and radio actor, script writer for radio and
television, playwright and novelist; his six novels which have
a South African setting are:* The Goddam White Man;
A Place Apart; The Paradise People; The Grass
Won't Grow till Spring; The Freedom of the Cage;
and A Tale of Love, Alas.

CHARACTERS

Adelaide, } 2 elderly spinsters.
Edith,
Gorman, *a Special Branch (white) policeman.*
The Man, *an African in his early thirties, a politico.*
Wanjiro, *Foreman in carpentry shop.*
Manager, *in carpentry shop.*
Voice, *on telephone switchboard.*
Nurse.

For John Ryder

SCENE ONE

The verandah of the farm belonging to Adelaide and Edith. Doves and bees can be heard in the background.

ADELAIDE : All afternoon the little man sat with us, here on the verandah.

EDITH : From one thirty to five fifteen. Saying very little.

ADELAIDE : But most peculiar, conveying a great deal.

GORMAN : Did he say where he had come from? I must have these facts.

ADELAIDE : He mentioned hills to the north.

EDITH : He was not precise.

ADELAIDE : He did say he had come down from the hills. In the north; but that did not seem important enough to pursue. There was so much else.

GORMAN : What else?

EDITH : I do not think my friend would be able to say.

ADELAIDE : I did say later, my dear, it could have been as if two worlds had got themselves mixed or momentarily tangled.

EDITH : That would not help the police.

GORMAN : Anything can help, if only to eliminate or confirm. Which two worlds, ma'am?

ADELAIDE : As if a madonna stepped out of a picture and started to dress the baby. Or Mr Pickwick dropped in to tea. Those two worlds, ours and theirs, getting mixed.

GORMAN : You say you sat here, on the verandah?

EDITH : As we are sitting now.

GORMAN (*gentle*): Is that usual, to invite a strange man up here, on your verandah? A native.

ADELAIDE: Nothing is usual out here. There is very little repetition.

EDITH: And we did not precisely invite him. He came up the steps and knocked at the double door there. Adelaide was in the long room labelling the honey pots. I was back in the scullery cleaning the separator.

ADELAIDE: I heard the knocking, which was gentle, and thought at last we should have a breeze. It has been so stifling and the thought of freshness made me begin to sing.

EDITH: Although we are high up here, the mountains fold us in. The breeze, as it were, must come from above. It must pour over and down.

ADELAIDE: The stillness is what decided us, twenty-five years ago next month.

GORMAN: But then you realized it was a knock.

ADELAIDE: Because it was repeated, rhythmically, and with the artificial intervals the breeze does not imitate.

EDITH: And I heard it too and came out, drying my hands, and believe, Ady, I saw him first, framed in the doorway and quite startlingly solid because of the intense glare, you understand, behind him.

ADELAIDE: It was more or less midday. That great mass of trees out there on the slope tilt the light directly at us. Like millions of tiny mirrors, the leaves.

EDITH: I said, 'Yes, can I help you?'

ADELAIDE: And I came forward to see and saw him, and was considerably startled that he was so small and frail. The natives we mostly see are magnificent . . .
Gorman utters a slight cough.

ADELAIDE: Specimens. Oh yes, they are.

EDITH: And he had shoes on.

ADELAIDE: They don't generally.

EDITH: Quite out of place. They were two-toned sporting shoes.

GORMAN: Ah.

ADELAIDE: White fronts, or they had been white.

EDITH: Red dust from the red road you came in by.

ADELAIDE: And, I suppose, dark tan the rest might have been.

EDITH: And I said, 'Yes, can I help you?'

ADELAIDE: We both stood together just there and he looked so small, and dusty. I thought then how he might be all dust.

GORMAN: What did he say? (*slight pause*)
What did he say?

ADELAIDE: Well, now let me think – Oh, yes . . .
Slight pause with slightly different background sounds.

THE MAN: Could I have some water, please?

EDITH: Most certainly. Ady, would you cut up a lemon while I get the water. I'll bring it to you on the verandah. Do sit down. Would you like some, Ady?

ADELAIDE: Please. A slice of lemon in a glass of water is very refreshing. The wicker chair is the most comfortable.

THE MAN: Thank you.
Longish pause.

ADELAIDE: Yes. (*slight pause*) Everything at a point of rest, poised, before we go on towards dark. It is hard to think of the dark in this bright noonday glare. And hard, in the dark, to recapture noonday.
Pause.

ADELAIDE: You are a long way from anywhere, here.

THE MAN: I am on my way. To Karendu.

ADELAIDE (*laughs*): What a peculiar way. Karendu is twenty-five miles to the south.

EDITH (*offstage*): Are you doing the lemon, dear?

ADELAIDE: Oh my! Do excuse me a moment.

THE MAN: Thank you.
Edith brings in the glass.

EDITH: Had you forgotten already? You are getting scatter-brained, Ady, getting much worse.

ADELAIDE: I won't be a moment.

EDITH: Here we are, but we must wait for lemon. Please do sit down. You look worn out. I cannot imagine where you could have come from to pass this way which is so out of the way.

THE MAN: From the north. Over the mountains. It is a short cut.

EDITH: Over the mountains? In those shoes?

THE MAN: Oh no. These are just for approaching. Bare-feet in the mountains.
Adelaide comes back.

DELAIDE: Edith, you left the cool cupboard door open.

EDITH: Did I?

ADELAIDE: I'm not the only scatterbrain, dear.

EDITH: It's so easy. The silence plays tricks. And age, I
suppose. I caught myself standing I don't know
how long yesterday, staring at a plum. If it was
yesterday.
Adelaide pours the water, three glasses.

ADELAIDE: There we are.

THE MAN: Thank you. (*starts sipping*)

EDITH: I think you will find the lemon slices add just that
tang. Thank you, my dear. Our own lemons, you
know.

ADELAIDE: Those are all our trees out there. Lemon,
plum, pear, orange grove, but that you can't see
from here, and, our glory of glories, six persimmon
trees. People come from all over Africa to see them.

EDITH: We understand they are the only ones in Africa.
Miss Cranston's father was a sea captain and he
brought them from Japan and everyone said they
would never grow but we found them exactly the
right spot.

ADELAIDE: The fruit is just over or we could offer you
the taste.

EDITH: We have bread and cheese and fruit. We are not
flesh eaters.

ADELAIDE: You are most welcome.

EDITH: When you are rested. He has come over the
mountains.

ADELAIDE: How strange. I think I told you I dreamt of
someone walking on the mountain. Or did I say I
thought I saw someone. Up there on the skyline.

EDITH: When was that, dear?

ADELAIDE: I thought I did mention it.

EDITH: I cannot recall. We even lose touch with each other, let alone ourselves. The shapes melt away.

ADELAIDE: It's so peaceful, you understand. And there are no constraints, do you know what I mean, no frets, no impositions . . . you see how easily I can slip into rhapsody.

EDITH: Miss Cranston loves words. It is an entirely sensual love.

ADELAIDE: But I do believe sometimes, on these warm still days, that I might have already died, without noticing the event, it is so unimaginably peaceful. But surely you must be hungry, yes, and we have figs, quite enormous purple figs. You would like to wash, no doubt; let me show you the bathroom. Edith, would you like to bring out some fruit and bread? The shower, alas, is broken in some mysterious way we cannot discover.

THE MAN: Perhaps I may be able to mend it for you.

EDITH: We should be grateful, certainly, in this weather.

ADELAIDE: Come along. And do feel free to take your shoes off if you wish. They look hideously uncomfortable.
Pause, then back to the present.

GORMAN: I see. So he asked for water, stood there, and then you actually had him sitting here drinking the water . . .

ADELAIDE: As you are now, with lemon slices . . .

GORMAN: And what did you talk about, if you talked?

EDITH: Did we talk, dear?

ADELAIDE: I suppose we passed some remark or other.

GORMAN: What did he say?

EDITH: He said nothing.

GORMAN: What did you talk about?

ADELAIDE: Oh, nothing really.

GORMAN: Do you always invite such people to eat with you?

ADELAIDE: Such people? Such as what?

GORMAN: Natives, Miss Cranston. It is not the custom.

ADELAIDE: Oh. We didn't know that, did we dear?

EDITH: We are grateful for people. They are an event. We lose our sense of time. Events mark it out for us.

ADELAIDE: But I am so curious why you should be so interested in our little man, and to have come all this way to ask these questions.

GORMAN: It is part of an enquiry.

EDITH: He mended our shower most expertly, if that is any help.

GORMAN: I should like to examine that.

ADELAIDE: Oh, it works perfectly, now.

EDITH: What is the extraordinary interest in the little man? All this way to ask about him, it is so puzzling.

GORMAN: He is a very puzzling man. I can only tell you this. We have known about him . . . I have known about him . . . for quite a long time. But we have never . . . I have never . . . set eyes on him and the descriptions vary, not by much, but significantly. He travels . . . always, it seems, on foot . . . covering great distances by unusual routes and then he arrives at a place and stays there and something happens. Or rather, let me put it this way, wherever something happens, we discover he has been there. That is one question, naturally, which interests the authorities; and the other, of course, much simpler, is simply how he manages to travel and enter towns and get employment of some kind and leave again without a passbook. In that way he breaks the law. But how he manages it . . . it is almost impossible . . . we cannot imagine. He has obviously a great ability to take people in. He took you in.

EDITH: I beg your pardon.

GORMAN: No, no, he did. He's a dangerous man.

ADELAIDE (*gaily*): Oh, but so are you, are you not, and we serve you water from the same glass he drank from.

EDITH: He did not take us in. We took him in. But what happens at these places, what sort of thing happens?

GORMAN: That's just it, there is no particular pattern. Sometimes all the natives in the place stay away from work for a day or sometimes two or three days. That is against the law, as you know.

EDITH: We did not.

GORMAN: Sometimes they all go to the local church, the white church, where they are not allowed, on a Sunday and stand outside through the service, singing.

ADELAIDE: Oh, I should love to hear that.

GORMAN: But this time it is much more serious. And I want you, please, to listen to me very carefully because this time lives have been involved . . .

ADELAIDE: Involved?

GORMAN: Lost, lives have been lost and property destroyed, and that you will agree is a very serious matter and whatever anybody feels about the perpetrator, however charming or pathetic he can make himself, nevertheless, he has caused lives to be lost and property to be destroyed and that must be stopped – and the only way to stop it is to catch him.

EDITH: Captain Gorman, you seem to fear that we fail to understand you. We are not quite the children you seem to be addressing.

ADELAIDE: We know right from wrong.

GORMAN: Then forgive me; but you see I believe this man will impose on you again. He is hurt, he was wounded, he cannot get far without recovering from those wounds and, I believe, this is where he will come. I have not got enough men to watch every possible approach. If I put a man in here . . .

ADELAIDE: Goodness gracious me!

GORMAN: He would not come – and I want him to come, and I rely on you to tell me and to keep him here until I arrive.

EDITH: But how shall we tell you, Captain? We have no means.

GORMAN: I know that and I have brought the means. I have brought you two of my own pigeons. They are racing birds that I breed. When he arrives you will release the one with two rings on its foot and if he leaves immediately you will release the other.

The birds will reach my loft within half an hour. I
can be here inside an hour. So you see, I only need
at the most, two hours . . . for you to keep him two
hours.

EDITH: But you have not said what he has done or
whether indeed there is proof he did it. We should
want to know that.

GORMAN: He came to Karendu from here. There is a
furniture factory which employs all native labour.
It is subsidized by the government. We are teaching
the natives how to run their own little industries,
you understand. It is working . . . or was working
. . . most successfully. I have some of the furniture
they make in my own house. The manager is, or
was, he is dead now . . . a very decent African. He
can quote Shakespeare and people like that. He
could. Then the little man arrives. There are several
different episodes to what follows. I will try to make
them clear. He arrives and sees the manager.

SCENE TWO

A carpentry shop in a town near the farm.

THE MAN: You know me.

MANAGER: I know you.

THE MAN: You are sure. There are many that pretend to
be me.

MANAGER: I am sure. This is the foreman. He will show
you what work you can do while you are here. You
will stay in my house. Come here when work is
finished.

FOREMAN: You have done this work?

THE MAN: I know the work.

FOREMAN: Then come.
> *They go into the work area of the shop where the noise suddenly ceases.*

FOREMAN: Here at this bench. (*raising his voice*) Go on with your work now. Say nothing.
> *Work starts again, voice and chorus singing African national anthem into triumphant climax. A pause follows. Foreman dials a telephone number, five figures.*

VOICE: Police.

FOREMAN (*furtive*): Captain Gorman please.

VOICE: Who wants him?

FOREMAN: Wanjiro.

VOICE: Hold on.

GORMAN: Wanjiro?

FOREMAN: He has come.

GORMAN: What is the plan?

FOREMAN: There are people to be got out for the north.

GORMAN: Which people?

FOREMAN: I don't know.

GORMAN: How?

FOREMAN: Don't know.

GORMAN: When?

FOREMAN: Don't know. But he is here. At the factory.

GORMAN: Find out more. Let me know. Your money will be in the usual place.
> *Pause.*

MANAGER: Eight men is a lot.

THE MAN (*whispering*): They are willing. They are needed. This is the timetable. By train on the Friday to this point, by van on the Saturday to here and then across on the Sunday by lorry. All these will be in place.

MANAGER: But they cannot travel by train.

THE MAN: You have got an order by post for ten coffins . . .

MANAGER: Yes, from Pietersburg.

THE MAN: Eight of them you will make to this plan. The other two, normal.

MANAGER: Yes. That is good. Yes. Very good. But there is one thing. That Friday is the Easter holiday.

THE MAN: Exactly. The order is urgent. The men from here, therefore, will load the coffins. It is a matter of the weight, you see. At the other end, the same. Our men there.

MANAGER: We'll get on with making these then. Friday! Yes, it's good.
Pause.
Acoustic changes to telephone.

FOREMAN (*Off*): Friday. At the goods yard.

GORMAN: And will he be there?

FOREMAN: Yes, baas.

GORMAN: And you?

FOREMAN: Yes, baas.

GORMAN: Stay close to him and hold him when we show up.

FOREMAN: No, baas. That I cannot do.

GORMAN: You must. He is the one we want.

FOREMAN: Can't do it, baas. They would kill me.

GORMAN: We'll be there.

FOREMAN: No baas. Sorry. That I cannot do.

GORMAN: Listen, you know sedition is not the way, this is not the way for your people, makes trouble for everybody, and this is the man causing all that, making armies over the border. He always slips. You hold him for us. That'll be double for you. I'll double the money.

FOREMAN: No, no boss. Sorry. They'll kill me.

GORMAN: Treble, three times, then.

FOREMAN: No, baas. No.
Foreman rings off.

GORMAN: Hey, are you there? Wanjiro? (*sigh*)

SCENE THREE

Verandah of the farmhouse. Turtle doves can be heard.

GORMAN (*sighs*): So we had to rush them and we had him, for a few moments we had him, but he's got some strange hold over them and when they saw, they just went mad, there were dozens of them there. They picked up anything, sticks, stones, and charged. There were only six of us. About thirty, thirty-five of them. We had to open fire. Terrible. Terrible. We've never had trouble. They are good men. The manager, Mr Kunene, he was a friend of mine, a good man, three nice little boys, always very clean and well dressed. Now he's in one of his own coffins. What chance have those three little boys got now? *Pause.*

ADELAIDE: Listen. All the birds have stopped.

EDITH : That must be the hawk back again. Yes, there it is, the brute, over the woods.

ADELAIDE : We've never had hawks here before. Now this one has started regular visits and we don't know what to do to scare him off.

GORMAN : Yes, he's too high to shoot. Lammervanger. Big fellow. I can try and fix you up a trap . . .

ADELAIDE : Oh no, no, no, we couldn't trap it, no, that would be unpardonable. Just look at its sweeps. Arrogant devil.

EDITH : Might it not attack your pigeons, supposing we did release them? I don't say we will.

GORMAN : No, unlikely. It goes for bigger game and those pigeons are fast, they just burn through the sky. You see, we must have this man. You see the trouble that follows him everywhere, innocent lives lost, it's terrible, really terrible, and nothing is accomplished! What is accomplished by all this?

ADELAIDE : I don't really think, Edith dear, we're capable of distinguishing in these quarrels. I think we must say no. Or at least we would have to tell him . . .

GORMAN : Oh no, no, that wouldn't do.

ADELAIDE : There are always two sides, you see, and argument between them and about them is endless, and in the long run, pointless. We came here, twenty-five years ago to escape just such argument which was really making our lives a misery, wasn't it, dear?

EDITH : We don't need to go into all that.

ADELAIDE : But you see, captain, we could have wasted so much of our short lives in that argument without ever deciding anything or, if we had, it wouldn't have made a tittle of difference to the world's affairs or other couples like ourselves who wanted to live in the way we did.

GORMAN: But this is politics, ma'am, and subversion and revolution, and that affects everybody. Next thing, you could have a black army coming over those mountains!

ADELAIDE: We couldn't provide refreshment for an army.

GORMAN: They'd take it.

EDITH: And if we betray this man to you, might not his friends come over the mountain and take their revenge?

GORMAN: We would naturally give you protection.

ADELAIDE: People around here? Oh no. And it would have to be for the rest of our lives, surely.

GORMAN: No, no. This thing will be stamped out very soon.

ADELAIDE: What a horrible word . . . stamped.

GORMAN: The natives don't want it. They want to live in peace and grow and develop along their own lines.

EDITH: Oh, these slogans. Anyway I must take the bread out of the oven. You must excuse me. I don't think we can promise anything. (*goes*)

GORMAN: I will leave the pigeons with you. This is their corn and you won't mind seeing their water is topped up. A handful of this once a day in the evening. I'll fetch them for you. (*goes out*)

ADELAIDE: Oh dear, what confusion.
Doves, bees, car door offstage.

GORMAN (*at distance approaching*): Come, come, my pretties. Don't worry. Papa won't leave you long. (*re-enters*) Here we are. And this is the catch, you just lift this and take the bird out and throw him up into the air.

ADELAIDE: Well.

GORMAN: Of course he mustn't see you doing it. Where shall I put them?

ADELAIDE: Oh put them down there for the time being. We cannot promise anything.

EDITH (*coming in*): Oh, captain, good, I thought you might have gone. Look I have brought you one of our loaves for a treat. Town bread is so anaemic.

GORMAN: Hum-yuh. Smells delicious.

ADELAIDE: He should have some of our butter to go with it.

GORMAN: Oh, no, now you mustn't . . .

ADELAIDE: Oh yes. Edith makes the bread. I make the butter, and the two are inseparable. No other butter will do.

GORMAN: This is so kind of you.

ADELAIDE: I'll fetch it for you. (*goes off*)

EDITH: And those are the birds? They look very conspiratorial. Not the least innocent. Have they done this work before?

GORMAN: No.

EDITH; I do not like this feeling of . . . . affairs. I do not like to have any importance. Once, long ago, we were quite literally persecuted. People plotted and intrigued and it was quite the most horrible thing

I have ever encountered. The people's faces, they changed out of all recognition. I should not like to look like they did.

GORMAN: Why was this?

EDITH: Because we were in love, captain. Because we loved each other. Would you believe it?

GORMAN: I see. Yes. Well. (*pause*)

EDITH (*sighs*): Yes.

GORMAN: Of course this is not a matter of love but of hate, and hate breeding hate, and people being killed, innocent people. I do hope you will think about that.

ADELAIDE (*approaching*): Here we are, and I have chosen you some of our figs. They are magnificent, I can assure you.

EDITH: You can bring the basket back when you call for the pigeons.

GORMAN: They are marvellous. What a size. My wife is mad about figs, too. You are so kind. I'll be back on Thursday. If not before. Please think about what I said. Goodbye now.

ADELAIDE: Goodbye.

EDITH: Goodbye.
Gorman goes off, then pause. Distant car door and car.

ADELAIDE: What was it that he said, dear?

EDITH: I was telling him about us and he said this was not a matter of love but of hate and killing. I am not inclined to trust him on such matters.

ADELAIDE: Whyever not? He struck me as an amiable man. Limited, but quite amiable.

EDITH : When his mouth smiled, his eyes did not. He
thought he was putting it over on us. Charming us,
laying it on with a shovel, too. And speaking to us
as though we only had the intelligence of children.

ADELAIDE : We were not all that honest with him, dear. I
didn't much like to catch his eye in case I gave
myself away. It's all so confusing, and our little
man has not been telling us the truth either.

EDITH : We had better go and see how he is.

ADELAIDE (*as they go*): I keep wondering what we shall
do if he dies.

EDITH : Bury him, dear . . . (*to an inner room*) Are you
awake?

THE MAN : Yes.

ADELAIDE : How are you feeling now?

THE MAN : It's still bleeding. I'm sorry. It's all through
the bandages and the sheet. I'm sorry.

EDITH : Let me look . . . Oh dear. There must be some
way to stop it. It's such an awkward place. You
know, I do think we must get a doctor.

THE MAN : No.

EDITH : You didn't quite tell us the truth, did you?

THE MAN : I didn't tell you lies.

EDITH : You didn't tell us everything.

THE MAN : No.

ADELAIDE : Well, never mind that. We must change those
bandages.

EDITH : Yes, but you told us this was a spear wound and
it isn't, it's a bullet and it must be inside you.

THE MAN: Yes. But there is nothing to do.

EDITH: Nonsense.

THE MAN: No. It's bleeding inside too. I just wanted to
be with kind people to die. You were kind people;
when I came I didn't want to just . . . die out there
in the bush . . . like an animal. I wanted to tell
you. . . .

ADELAIDE: I don't think the effort of talking can be
good. I'm going to get some more bandages. (*going*)

THE MAN: I was so frightened when I knew it was inside
me. Will you stay with me? I'm sorry about the
bed, the mattress.

EDITH: Don't be frightened. There is nothing to be
frightened of.

THE MAN: I am not a Christian.

EDITH: But my dear man, people died long before Christ
was born and some accommodation had to be
made for them, don't you see, after death. If there
is an afterdeath. And isn't it exciting to be finding
out; and if there isn't you won't know you don't
know it; there will be absolutely nothing. And that
does no-one any harm.

ADELAIDE (*re-entering*): This is our last roll, dear. We shall
have to cut things up, after this. I don't quite
know what. And I've brought the iodine. It will
hurt dreadfully. But it may stop the bleeding.

EDITH: I don't think we need bother him with all that.
There's nothing we can do.

ADELAIDE: Oh, I don't agree . . .

EDITH: No, no. He knows best and I've sat watching him
now and there's no doubt. It's unmistakable.

225

ADELAIDE: Oh dear.

THE MAN: Could I have water with lemon in it.

EDITH: Of course. I'll get it. And dear, sit here and speak of pleasant things. (*going*)

ADELAIDE: It seems you were betrayed.

THE MAN: Yes. One man. I don't know who.

ADELAIDE: The foreman.

THE MAN: Ah yes. He smiled a lot. It is always like that. One man does not believe.

ADELAIDE: But surely it is not good to cause these disturbances.

THE MAN: So many things are not good. You are lucky. You live outside it all. We can't all do that.

ADELAIDE: No. And it is all quite beyond me. I'm no good at thinking. I never was. I see pictures when I think I'm thinking. Everything is pictures for me, and poetry. I hear poetry; it sings in my head around the pictures. You would think I was completely dotty and to tell the truth I don't know, not positively, whether I am dotty or not. Would you like me to read to you?

THE MAN: No. I'm frightened. I'm so frightened.

ADELAIDE: There, there. (*distressed*) Oh dear, what does one do? (*pause*) Here, hold my hand. (*pause*) 'Courage, he said and pointed toward the land. This mounting wave will roll us shoreward soon. In the afternoon, they came unto a land in which it seemed always afternoon. All round the coast the languid air did swoon, breathing like one that hath a weary dream. Full faced above the valley stood the moon like a downward smoke the something stream along the cliff to fall and pause and fall did seem. A land of streams. Some, like a downward smoke . . .'

EDITH (*approaching*): Here we are.

ADELAIDE: Sssh. He's asleep.
Edith sets down tray with glass and jug.

EDITH: Yes. Well, that's that.

ADELAIDE: Do you mean he's gone. Goodness gracious me. There wasn't a sound. I can hardly believe it. Well, well. How extraordinary.

EDITH: Yes, well now, my dear, we can release those blessed pigeons.

ADELAIDE: Both of them would mean he came and went.

EDITH: Well, that in a sense is what he has done.

ADELAIDE: But I think he should stay. I think we should bury him. Down by the persimmon trees.

EDITH: My dear, we would have to dig a very large hole, it's quite beyond us.

ADELAIDE: No it isn't. I insist. I want him to remain here. If they came they'd treat him like some carcass and probably throw him into quicklime . . . No, I insist. Goodness me, to go just like that. There wasn't a sound.

EDITH: And we'd have to get him down there. No, Ady, we couldn't possibly.

ADELAIDE: Of course we can. Look at him, he's only skin and bone. We could use that board in the barn as a stretcher as we do with the apple boxes. Lord, we've carried more than his weight up from the

orchard. Come along. If we release both birds they'll
go off looking for him somewhere and that should
give us plenty of time.
*Goes through the house and out to verandah. Pigeons
released. Whirr of wings.*

ADELAIDE: Wouldn't it be beautiful if we could both go
together, like that. I don't want to be left, darling, I
couldn't bear that, I think. I would have to come
on immediately. Oh my darling, my darling.

EDITH: I know. I know. And we haven't done anything
about it. We must. We must make written arrangements. Or they will take us away and bury us in
some wretched little ornamented cemetery.

ADELAIDE: There will eventually be three of us here.
Isn't that extraordinary? I wonder what they will
think about the third grave, what story they will
invent to account for it?

EDITH: Come along. We don't know that we can dig it
yet. It has to be deep.

ADELAIDE: And we'll need that old brown blanket.

SCENE FOUR

A garden near a stream on the farm.

EDITH: For as much as it has pleased Almighty God of
his great mercy to take unto himself the soul of our
dear brother here departed, we therefore commit his
body to the ground; earth to earth, ashes to ashes,
dust to dust, in sure and certain hope of the Resurrection to eternal life, through our Lord Jesus
Christ, who shall change our vile body that it may
be like his glorious body according to the mighty
working whereby he is able to subdue all things to
himself . . . There. I don't think we need say the
prayer.

228

ADELAIDE: No. You read it very beautifully, my dear.

EDITH: Well now we'd better . . .

ADELAIDE: Yes.
They begin shovelling soil.

SCENE FIVE

The verandah of the farm; sound of car approaching.

ADELAIDE (*calls*): Edith. Come, Edith. It's that man.

EDITH (*approaching*): Ah yes. Well. We know what to say.

GORMAN (*approaching*): Morning . . . morning, isn't it a loverlee morning. How are you both?

EDITH: Very well, thank you.

GORMAN: I hope it wasn't too much of a strain. My wife, you know, she was very angry with me, leaving you two out here with a desperate man on the run but I told her . . . I said . . . 'He won't harm them, he's not that kind, and they can . . .' how shall I say . . . there's something about you two good ladies . . . I said to her, 'Vera, those two could make a lion lie down quietly and purr.'

ADELAIDE: Oh dear me, how extravagant.

GORMAN: No, no. It's the peace – it's a sort of, like a kind . . . kind of yes a kind of a . . . halo round you, and round this place. My, it's so peaceful! Anyway, thank you so much. I can't tell you how much.

EDITH: But there's nothing to thank us for, captain.

GORMAN: Oh yes. You know, quite honestly, I thought that you wouldn't, and then I thought and I said to my wife, 'They are sensible people, they'll see, they'll see the issues and they'll do the right thing!'

and as soon as those two birds arrived . . . well it
was just a matter of the old hunter's instinct, hey?
guessing which way he would go out and being
there and there he was and we picked him up. All
in the bag.
Pause.

ADELAIDE: You *picked* him *up*?

GORMAN: Well, it's a manner of speaking. Arrested him.
And the other three. I don't know if they came here.
But they were with him. Of course he was very
badly wounded, in the side here, as you know and
it's probably, well, he probably won't pull through,
I don't think.

EDITH: You are perfectly sure it was him?

GORMAN: Right down to the two-tone shoes you described.

EDITH: A small man.

GORMAN: Yes, a comparatively, yes, I would . . . there's
no doubt at all.

ADELAIDE: The foreman identified him, no doubt.

GORMAN: Well, no, he's . . . he's disappeared.

EDITH: How extraordinary.

GORMAN: Scared, I suppose.

ADELAIDE: He would have need to be.

EDITH: It really is most extraordinary.

GORMAN: There seems to be something worrying you.

ADELAIDE: No. No. It's just . . .

EDITH: What time did you find him?

GORMAN: Oh it was about half past five I think, yes, half past five.

ADELAIDE: I see. That was about three hours, Edith, wasn't it?

EDITH: Yes, three hours almost exactly.

GORMAN: Well . . . I'll just collect my basket and I've brought you yours, so we'll sort of swap baskets, hey? and I'll toddle off. My wife has put in here just a little of her quince jelly that she makes that she thought you might like to try because those figs . . . I can't begin to tell you . . .

EDITH: How very kind of her. We both adore quince jelly, don't we, dear.

ADELAIDE: You must thank her most particularly.

GORMAN: Oh, it's our pleasure . . . Well . . . You mustn't worry about it. Honestly . . . You are worrying about it, aren't you?

EDITH: Yes, I don't think it can be the same man. You see, we have those shoes. . . fetch them, dear, will you? . . . He left them here.

GORMAN: Well . . . I don't know. This is very puzzling.

EDITH: Indeed it is.

GORMAN: I don't know. No, I really don't know. Except to ask you to come in and identify him. I'll take you in and bring you back.

EDITH: Yes. Yes. I would be most curious.

ADELAIDE: These are his shoes.

GORMAN: Well. Not quite the same, certainly. More or less. I don't know. I mean there isn't all that number of natives walking about with two-tone shoes, hey?

EDITH: We will come with you. Just give us a few moments, will you?

GORMAN: Yes, yes, surely. I'll just go and turn the car. Collect my basket. (*going off*)
Adelaide and Edith enter house.

ADELAIDE: Whatever does it mean?

EDITH: I can't think. But it can't be the same man.

ADELAIDE: But the shoes?

EDITH: Perhaps there was some plan to provide a decoy or something like that . . . I don't know, dear. We must just go and see and pray . . .

ADELAIDE: Pray for what?

EDITH: Pray that we say and do the right thing. I think I'll take my purse. There are one or two things we need, so we might as well take this opportunity.

ADELAIDE: We need more bandages.

EDITH: Yes, I want a pair of kitchen scissors.

ADELAIDE: Oh, and string, one of those large balls of string . . .

SCENE SIX

The receptionist's desk, passage and morgue of the town's hospital.

GORMAN: Ah, nurse, these two ladies have come along, very kindly, to identify the prisoner.

NURSE: He's gone.

GORMAN: Gone, what do you mean, gone?

NURSE: He died about two hours ago. He's in the mortuary.

GORMAN: Oh . . . Well . . . Still . . . Could I ask you?

EDITH: Yes.

NURSE: Do you want to see him?

GORMAN: Yes, please.

NURSE: Come this way, will you?
They go into mortuary.

NURSE (*approaching body*): Here. He hasn't been washed yet.

GORMAN: Well? Is it?

EDITH: Yes.

ADELAIDE: Oh yes, that's the man.

GORMAN: Well . . . I don't know. Maybe he had . . . well you don't carry around two pairs of shoes like that?

EDITH: Perhaps they do.

GORMAN: But you are quite sure this is the man.
Pause.

EDITH: Apart from what death does . . .

GORMAN: There is a change, yes. And you didn't see the other three who were with him? We've got them down at the station.

ADELAIDE: Oh no, there was nobody else.

EDITH: Nobody. We . . . er . . .

GORMAN: Oh yes, I'm sorry. Yes. Not a very pleasant place. This way . . . Now, you want to do some shopping first.

EDITH: The wife and the three little boys of the manager you said quoted Shakespeare . . .

233

GORMAN: Yes?

EDITH: As you know, we have a large place and could quite easily build on to it.

GORMAN: Would you like to see her now?

EDITH: I think so, don't you Ady. We could do with some help. And we have somehow become involved.

GORMAN: Oh, that would really be so marvellous. I have been so worried for them. They would grow up decent and no bitterness. That's what we want. We can't have this going on and on. Oh, that is something really good, really good.

ADELAIDE: If she wishes it.

GORMAN: Oh, I'm sure, I'm sure. What an opportunity. It's so beautiful and peaceful and . . . it's good, you feel good out there. You are good people, good people. Yes.

ADELAIDE: Well, we have somehow become . . . involved.

GORMAN: You'll like her, you'll like her very much I'm sure. We'll go now. It's not far. Just down the street.

SCENE SEVEN

A room at the farm, turtledove background.

ADELAIDE: He was in a way rather like, don't you think?

EDITH: Very. Most extraordinary.

ADELAIDE: It was quick of you to say yes. I did not know what was best to say.

EDITH: I don't know why I said yes . . . Don't light the lamp yet, darling. We'll have all the moths in.

ADELAIDE: I was going to close the wire door.

EDITH: Don't, not yet. There is just the faintest breeze.

ADELAIDE: She seems very nice, a soft little thing. But I don't know the least about little boys. I fear things will be broken.

EDITH: Oh, we shall be very firm. That is what one must be, Ady, with boys. Firm. Then we have gentlemen. And three more gentlemen in the world is not too much. But it's all such a tease. I can't help thinking . . . (*pause*)

ADELAIDE: I've been thinking too. It's really rather comforting. When things don't make immediate and mundane sense. As though one must try to see behind them. There's something more. Mysterious . . . (*pause*)

EDITH: It's such a puzzle. (*pause*)

ADELAIDE: And lo, I am with you always, even unto the end of the world.
Pause.

EDITH: Those doves are singing late.

ADELAIDE: Oh, I could sing for ever, now that I know. Just know.

EDITH: Yes. Well. We can't go on sitting here in the dark. And we had better start getting things ready for tomorrow. They'll be here before we know it. Light the lamp now, darling, will you?

CURTAIN

1. *ANCESTRAL POWER*

Originally written as a play for radio.

ONE SCENE: Set near a Ghanaian village, in modern times.

Akoto's big talk and long boastfulness about himself and his forebears is brought to an abrupt end when the police appear.

2. *THE MAGIC POOL*

A stage play.

ONE SCENE: set near a Kenyan village in modern times.

The loneliness and longings of a deformed boy who, already set apart from his age-mates in the village, is taunted by a youth from the city – can there be solace in a vision that he becomes aware of in the 'magic' pool?

3. *GOD'S DEPUTY*

A stage play.

Act 1: the Pavilion of the Gahmororo Palace, W. Nigeria.
Act 2: Bashorun's Compound.
Act 3: As for First Act.
Time: Late Nineteenth Century.

A Yoruba King is vastly angered when a favourite daughter refuses to marry according to her father's kingly dictates. In a play which sustains tension through scenes of sudden, surprising and explosive emotion, there is also controlling humour, ceremony and a logic of personality, station and background.

God's Deputy was written with its production in the form

of an opera in view. The present play, then, though amenable to reading and production away from its original musical conception can also be regarded as the libretto for the opera on which Sanya Dosunmu initially collaborated with AKIN EUBA, the Nigerian musicologist, musician and composer.

4. *RESURRECTION*

A stage play.

ONE SCENE: an empty dining-room in a house in Cape Town; modern times.

Mavis relives scenes of her life with her late mother, who, in life, recognized the advantages that a light-coloured skin gave some of her children, and therefore pandered to the whims of whites and 'play-whites' in South Africa's colour-caste society.

This play is an adaptation, by the author himself, of his short story of the same name which appears, i.a., in his anthology *Modern African Prose*, Heinemann Educational Books, A.W.S. No. 9.

It was first performed on 9 and 30 April 1966 (with two other plays: *Broken Teacups* by Harmon S. Watson, and *The Pure Truth* by Iris Allen-David, under the direction of Edward de Roo, by the Department of Speech and Theatre Arts' Experimental Theatre, Univ. of Columbia, U.S.A., with Wougene Patterson playing the part of Mavis, the young 'Cape Coloured' girl in Cape Town, South Africa, in whose mind the action is 'set'. (information from *Cultural Events in Africa*, No. 19, May, 1966)

5. *LIFE-EVERLASTING*

A stage play.

ONE SCENE: A small, undecorated, unfurnished room in the house of the dead; time, the present.

238

Three people from quite different professional backgrounds, but with a surprising lot in common under the surface in certain traits of personality and social disposition, are thrown together after death to think over and puzzle out the meaning, the means and ends and end of their lives, and the texture, taste and shape of futures that await or surround and prove them.

Parts of this play were staged as alternate reading and straight production in London, with Valerie Murray, Cosmo Pieterse and Pat Maddy. A revised version of this play is being considered for production and publication.

6. *LAMENT*

A radio play.

ONE SCENE: The time and place are relatively indeterminate, but the setting is a generalized African one, and the period fairly contemporary.

A richly poetic elegy/litany in which mime, dance, movement, slides, silhouettes, and colour can be used in addition to the three voices, or the voices alone can be allowed to play out the drama of departure: departure from a beloved, from home, from the old ways, from oneself.

7. *BALLAD OF THE CELLS*

A play for radio, film or stage.

Main Setting: a police interrogation cell where Looksmart is being cross-questioned. As he recalls various scenes of his life, the shifts of background to the Transkei, Cape Town, Worcester, Pretoria, the Drakensberg range of mountains, the Johannesburg gold mines, the Vaal-river, etc, can be achieved through black-outs and slide projections in a stage production.

Looksmart Solwande Ngudle was one of the earliest
victims of the Republic of South Africa's 90-Day Law
of the early 1960's, under which anyone suspected of
subversive knowledge could be detained for indefinite
'90-day' periods, with no charges preferred, in solitary
confinement, for interrogation. Looksmart's eventual death
was officially ascribed to 'heart failure'.

8. *OVERSEAS*

A radio play.

SIX SCENES: set in the present time, chiefly in an African
village, near the north-west coast, not far from a river.
SCENE 1: late afternoon; the compound and inside of Ma
    Ndutu's hut.
SCENE 2: evening; a roadside hut by the river.
SCENE 3: a week later: Ma Ndutu's hut – inside.
SCENE 4: night; on the river, in a canoe.
SCENE 5: morning; a room in the house of a medicine
    man.
SCENE 6: Some time later: a room in a boarding-house in
    a European city.

A young man brings the old Ma Ndutu a letter from
her son who is a student overseas. This gives us the
interplay between her thoughts about, her recollections of,
and longing for her son on the one hand, and on the other
the nostalgia, the promise and faith that speak from the
letter he has written her.

Ma Ndutu is ailing; she seems to be dying. Ndongo,
the young girl 'betrothed' to the absent Muledi, overseas
– studying – tends to the needs of the old woman.
Neighbours discuss the son's prolonged stay so far away,
and the possible effects on his brain of all the study.

At home Ma Ndutu gets weaker; her son, overseas,
studying, grows stronger in the conviction that he must go
home and 'pay for wasted time'.

*First directed and produced by John Gordon for the
African Theatre series of the B.B.C. African Service.
First transmitted on Sunday 7 July 1968, 0815–0900 GMT,
and Tuesday 9 July 1968, 2030–2115 GMT.
Another, earlier version of this play, dated 17 January 1967,
is entitled 'Those in the Distance'.
Extracts from another version have been published in
African Arts/Arts d'Afrique (UCLA), last quarter, 1970;
it is the conclusion of the version published in the magazine
that is preferred by the author himself.*

9. *THIS TIME TOMORROW*

A stage play.

Set in the slum area outside an East African city, in the
present time, the action opens in a journalist's office, then
moves to the inside of Njango's shelter of rusting tin and
rotting cardboard. From then the action alternates between
the newspaper office and slum shanty, or an entire scatter
of lean-to's that represent a street-market/meeting place in
the slum.

All the simple folk of the country have struggled and
sacrificed and suffered for freedom, and now that it has
come they still have to contend with poverty, unemploy-
ment and squalor in the city slums. The city fathers have
decreed that the slums must be removed, entirely razed.
A stranger in the area about to be evacuated and bulldozed
promises to be a 'trouble-maker': he reminds the people
of their courage in the fight for Uhuru yesterday, he
points out to them what is visibly there: their plight of
the present, and he makes them ask what will be and where
will they themselves be 'this time tomorrow'.

A sound (radio) version of this play was first broadcast on
the B.B.C. African Service in the African Theatre series
during 1967.

10. *EPISODES OF AN EASTER RISING*

A radio play.

The action takes place near a South African town, probably in the Northern Transvaal (or just possibly in northern Natal), fairly near the South African border: a farm, rather isolated; time, the present.

Seven clearly defined scenes play off-on:

1 : the verandah of the farm belonging to Adelaide and Edith.
2 : a carpentry shop in a town near the farm.
3 : a room in the farmhouse.
4 : a garden near a stream on the farm.
5 : the verandah.
6 : the receptionist's desk, passage and morgue of the town's hospital.
7 : the farmhouse.

Does 'Easter Rising' here refer to the Christian resurrection, or to the rising of the spirit of rebellion like the Irish Easter Rising of the 1910's? The 'strange' love of the two women who live apart from the rest of society is strikingly used as a sign and signal of their ability to understand, most tellingly, the love that the (political) man feels for his oppressed people. They therefore accommodate him, harbour him and after his death bury him in pure compassion; in genuine humanity, and from a kind of hunger, they can adopt the (orphaned) children of Kunene, the carpentry shop's manager where the man once ordered coffins for his political work.

First produced by R. D. Smith for the B.B.C. Third Programme.

PB-07664
AS-24

PB-07464
5-24

PB-07984
3-84